Steampunk Tea Party

Steampunk Tea Party

From Cakes & Toffees to Jams & Teas
30 Neo-Victorian Steampunk Recipes
From Far-Flung Galaxies, Underwater
Worlds & Airborne Excursions

Jema *Emilly Ladybird* Hewitt

D&C
David and Charles
Cincinnati, OH

TABLE OF CONTENTS

Chapter One
ALL ABOARD THE AIRSHIP
Elegance   8

Built by Cornelius and Sylvester Day, this luxury airship boasts a tea room to rival the Ritz. An elegant orchestra plays as the ladies' lace tea gowns sweep down the gilded staircase into the observation lounge. Captains and Society beauties rub shoulders with clockwork creations.

MENU: Lavender Creams · Venusian Delight · Chocolate Elegance Scones · Gin and Tonic Cake · Airship Cake Pops

Chapter Two
THE SCIENTIFIC CHATEAU
30

High on a windswept plateau stands the Castle of Dr. Ruthven, an amateur cryptozoologist and his slightly sinister sister. Lost travelers are often suprised to find a splendid meal, served on bone china and crystal, waiting in the great hall, where medieval banners sway in the breeze.

MENU: Stripey Syringe Push Pops · Mysterious Monster Bites · Mechanical Box Cake · Volcano Toffee · Aetheric Iced Tea and Other Concoctions

Chapter Three
A CURIOUS PICNIC   54

What could be lovelier on a sunny day than a picnic? Surrounded by strange topiaries, high tea in an Alice-in-Wonderland style setting ensures Mr. Woppit's relations enjoy their crumpets in truly topsy turvey style from beautifully patterned but mismatched china.

MENU: Gingerbread Woppits · Strawberry and Rose Conserve · Tea Time Truffles · Tipsy Turvey Tea Bread · Magical Fruit Scones

Chapter Four
REGIMENTAL LUNAR ENCAMPMENT ON MARS
74

The first Lunar regiment on Mars marches on its stomach. Not literally, of course, that would be silly, but they do enjoy their tiffin in style. Crisp linen and smart uniforms and, of course, shining silverware are seen in this officers' mess tent tea party. Best not to mention the Martians.

MENU: Crumpet Moons · Lunar Regimental Chutney · Empire Rocket Cupcakes · Harlech Cakes · Pith Helmet Fancies

Chapter Five
VOYAGE FROM THE DEEPS
96

The engineers aboard Her Majesty's Submersible *Naughty Lass* appreciate a proper mug of tea and a slice of cake as they peruse the blueprints for the latest devices aboard ship. Giant octopi loiter hopefully at the portholes, reaching at the plate of cog biscuits held by Admiral Saunders.

MENU: Mr. Rivet's Cheese and Chili Scones · Admiral's Marmalade · Nautilus Ship Biscuits · Absinthe Cog Biscuits · Mr. Brunel's Favorite Fudge

Chapter Six
BLOSSOMS IN SHANGRI-LA
116

The Adventurers Club Tea House in Shangri-La provides a welcome respite from the hurley burley of the modern world. Perched high on a mountain side in the ruins of a Tibetan monastry, weary travelers may rest and enjoy an elegant tea ceremony amid the cherry blossom.

MENU: Adventurer's Breakfast Muffins · Tea Eggs · Oriental Gooseberry and Blackcurrant Fruit Cheese · Time Traveler's Tart · Pasha's Chai · Sherpa's Chestnuts · Pear, Parsnip and Rose Loaf Cake

INTRODUCTION

"THERE ARE FEW HOURS IN LIFE MORE AGREEABLE THAN THE HOUR DEDICATED TO THE CEREMONY KNOWN AS AFTERNOON TEA."

HENRY JAMES, *The Portrait of a Lady*

Nothing compares to a nice cup of tea accompanied by a cake or two and enjoyed with friends. Tea time is a moment to relax—a time to chat and exchange news and opinions. Steampunks are social creatures, and the Victorian afternoon tea has proved itself a firm favorite among their social engagements.

Tea drinking as a ritual first originated in ancient China, later spreading throughout the Orient in the elegant formal tea ceremonies of Japan. Europe was still in the Dark Ages, quaffing mead and small beer with no idea of what it might be missing! Fortunately, civilizing tea was eventually introduced to Europe by Dutch explorers in the 1600s. The English East India company would bring it to England as a gift for the wife of Charles II.

During the 1700s, tea, also called tay or chay, gradually replaced coffee as the British beverage of choice. Queen Catherine's preference for tea as the beverage of choice among courtiers popularized it as a drink suitable for both ladies and gentlemen. Soon, tea would outstrip silk as China's biggest export.

The Duchess of Bedford is credited with the invention of afternoon tea as a meal in the mid 1840s. Feeling rather peckish between her light midday luncheon and the elaborate evening dinner at Woburn Abbey, she took to having a cup of tea with a few little cakes and invited friends to partake. It is possible that Queen Victoria, whilst visiting, enjoyed this ritual, for as the idea spread it quickly became the most popular meal of the Victorian day, with the food becoming ever more exciting.

In perfect Steampunk serendipity, it was a machine that revolutionized fancy baking in the Victorian era. Gas-fired ranges were amongst the exhibits at the Great Exhibition in 1851. Although their popularity was not immediate, later models brought the technical aspects of baking ornate pastries and elaborate cakes, hitherto seen only in continental patisseries, well within the reach of the domestic cook.

So much for tea, you say, but what about Steampunk? Who are these Steampunks and why should we want to take tea with them? Well, Steampunk has been variously described as an art movement and a subculture, but what it boils down to is Victorian science fiction. It is a very general term used to describe a wide variety of activities, creations and people who share a common interest in blending the historical with the scientifically fantastical. It is often typified by a specific look of Victorian-styled clothing, brass pipes, gears and rivets into which historical elements, such as mahogany rayguns, short skirts, brass rockets and other imaginary steam- or clockwork-driven inventions are incorporated.

Steampunk design turns up in films such as Guy Ritchie's *Sherlock Holmes* and Luc Besson's *The Extraordinary Adventures of Adèle-Blanc Sec*. There are Steampunk bands, exhibitions, markets, books, art and conventions, all created and attended by those who love the genre. There are also tea parties galore, filled with tea and cake; chatting; sandwiches; dress up; biscuits; being creative; and don't forget scones!

If you enjoy some or all of the above, then I hope this book may help you release your inner Steampunk and share your adventures with family and friends. The different themes demonstrate different approaches to Steampunk; though, with a little tweaking, any recipe can be suitable for any occasion! Now, may I invite you to sit down with a nice cup of tea and accompany me on a wonderful adventure to Biscuits and Beyond!

Love,

Emilly Ladybird

8

CHAPTER ONE

ALL ABOARD THE AIRSHIP *Elegance*

Dear Lady Lyssa,

I am most taken with this luxury airliner mode of transportation, and I think you would enjoy it immensely, too. One's every wish is answered almost before the thought pops into one's head; like magic, a charming brass assistant appears to service your desires, whether it be a glass of something lovely or a pair of binoculars with which to view the sunset over Jupiter.

The dresses of the lady travelers are glorious, too. Fashions from every corner of the galaxy are represented; star motifs continue to be popular, as does Arcadian silk. Bustles seem to be bigger than ever, which can lead to some interesting impasses in the corridors. I have been collecting fashion magazines for you from every planet we call on and will send them en masse by the Mail when we get to Gemini Major.

I have been a little concerned about the proximity of air kraken once or twice, but there is so much to do on board the ship, quite apart from admiring the views, that any worries are soon driven quite away. Well, I must be off—I am taking tea this afternoon at the captain's table with a most convivial party!

Love,

Emilly

Captain Cornelius Day cordially invites you to join him for afternoon tea at his table in the Observation Lounge this afternoon at four (Lunar Time).

There will be ample time to admire the Venusian Borealis, a rare display of exotic lights across the planet's atmosphere, and do bring your opera glasses as there may be a chance to spot an air kraken or two on their annual migration!

RSVP

All Aboard the Airship
Elegance Tea Menu

LAVENDER CREAMS

VENUSIAN DELIGHT

CHOCOLATE ELEGANCE SCONES

GIN AND TONIC CAKE

AIRSHIP CAKE POPS

STEAMER B GIN TEA COCKTAILS

– ALSO CONSIDER SERVING –

EGG MAYONNAISE WITH CRESS SANDWICHES

FINE SLICED CUCUMBER SPRINKLED WITH
VINEGAR SANDWICHES

EARL GREY TEA

LAVENDER CREAMS

Dainty debutantes are supposed to sit still for hours, having their hair curled while admiring the view of the outer moons from the luxury of their state cabins. They are not supposed to gallivant about enjoying themselves!

Abandoning her plate of lavender creams, Miss Honeykirk had slipped away from her chaperone for only a minute when the sounds of a jolly country dance seemed to beckon her down the filigree stairwell to the part of the ship she had been warned never to venture into. The noise of revelry grew louder; the sound of dancing feet and cheers was quite unlike anything she had encountered on the elegant dance floors of Elara or Sinope. A laughing couple pushed past her, hand in hand, swinging the door open and enticing Miss Honeykirk to join the dance.

Ingredients

FOR THE BISCUITS

20g (¾ oz.) icing sugar

15–30g (1-2 tbsp.) fresh lavender flowers (according to taste) or 8–15g (½–1 tbsp.) of dried lavender

100g (3½ oz.) plain flour

25g (1 oz.) instant custard powder

90g (3¼ oz.) butter

FOR THE LAVENDER FILLING

50g (1¾ oz.) unsalted butter, softened

80g (2½ oz.) icing sugar, sifted

A few drops of lavender-flavored essence

1–3 drops of purple food coloring

*Makes 8 sandwiched biscuits

PANTRY PERFECTIONS

If you would like to make these biscuits when lavender is not in flower, it's very easy to dry some of your own.

· Cut the lavender on its long stalk just as it flowers.

· Add 2.5g (½ tsp.) of salt to a basin of water and mix until the salt dissolves.

· Immerse the flower heads in the water and swish about for a bit to get rid of any bugs.

· Shake off excess water and tie the stalks into a bunch using ribbon. Place a muslin bag over the whole bouquet, flower end first, gathering the opening around the stalks to prevent it from getting dusty or shedding flowers as it dries.

· Hang the bouquet somewhere warm and dark like an airing cupboard. Allow the bouquet to hang until it is completely desiccated.

· Carefully undo the bag over a large sheet of paper, and gently rub the flowers from the woody stem.

· Use the paper to pour the dry flowers into an airtight jar, where they will keep very well for months.

TO MAKE THE BISCUITS

1 Preheat the oven to gas mark 4 (350° F/180° C) and grease a baking tray.

2 Place the icing sugar and lavender flowers in a food processor and blitz for 30 seconds until the lavender is fully incorporated into the sugar. There may still be flecks of flowers, which is fine, but you'll want to avoid leaving big chunks of flowers in the mixture.

3 Add the flour, custard powder and butter into the food processor. Blitz the mixture until it produces fine crumbs and then forms into a ball. Stop as soon as the mixture has become a nice dough ball. Leave to chill for 30 minutes in the refrigerator.

4 Roll the dough out on a floured board to about 2.5mm (¹⁄₁₆"–¹⁄₈") thickness. Cut out sixteen 2" (5cm) rounds. Cut out mini shapes from the centers of 8 of the rounds. These will be the top biscuits.

5 Place all the biscuits on the greased baking tray and bake for 10–12 minutes.

6 Remove the biscuits from the oven and allow to cool on the tray for 1 minute in order to firm up. Transfer to a wire rack to cool completely.

To Make the Lavender Filling

1 With an electric mixer, beat the softened butter and sifted icing sugar together with the essence and food coloring. Adjust the flavor to taste and the color to preference.

To Finish

1 Once the biscuits have cooled completely, spread a layer of lavender cream on top of the solid biscuits. Then, gently press 1 cut out biscuit on top of the spread, creating 8 sandwich biscuits.

PANTRY PERFECTIONS

When making sandwich biscuits with cutouts, it's best to use simple, bold shapes that will showcase the vibrantly colored icing. In addition to the obvious cookie cutter shapes available to bakers, like stars or hearts, you can find unusual miniature cutters in the baking section of craft stores. You can also combine basic shapes to create something unique. For example, you could use a square and a thin rectangle to make a top hat.

For special designs, such as initials, make a template to place on your biscuit rounds, then carefully cut around the design with a sharp scalpel or craft knife.

Venusian Delight

If a gentleman is looking for a small gift to present to his Lady before the on-board entertainment of opera or, perhaps, a play, he could do far worste than a box of this most elegant of confectionaries. Imagine, if you will, the airship's opulent theatre—the gold leaf and velvet curtains, the clusters of cherubs wrestling with air kraken high above in the tromp-l'oeil ceiling. The lady surveys the room with her opera glasses and turns to the dashing gentleman beside her, who, like a magician, produces his prize.

The little gasp of pleasure as the shape of the box is recognized, the perusal of the picture and the happy sigh as the first piece is tasted are sure to give any gentleman a warm glow. Of course, after consuming the entire box, the lady is also likely to glow and insist on singing all the arias on the way back to her cabin!

TO MAKE THE DELIGHT

1 Line a 7" × 4" (18cm × 10cm) loaf tin with foil. Oil well with 5ml (1 tsp.) of sunflower or olive oil.

2 Add granulated sugar and 70ml (2½ fl. oz.) of water to a saucepan and heat on a very low flame, stirring with a wooden spoon until all the sugar is dissolved. The result should be a syrupy mixture.

3 Bring the mixture to a boil, up to 240° F (115° C) on a sugar thermometer. Remove the pan from heat as soon as it reaches this temperature.

4 In a second saucepan, add corn flour and icing sugar, then add 300ml (½ pt.) of water a little at a time, stirring until fully blended.

Once thoroughly blended, gently heat the mixture, stirring continuously with a wooden spoon to prevent lumps from forming. Continue to heat until the mixture thickens like glue. If it becomes lumpy, remove from the heat and beat until the lumps are absorbed.

Keep heating and stirring until the mixture can get no thicker, about 1–2 minutes.

5 Pour the first syrupy mixture very slowly into the second mixture, incorporating it little by little and stirring all the time to mix evenly and avoid any lumps.

HOUSEKEEPER'S PERKS

If you're feeling adventurous, or if absinthe proves hard to come by, you could try any of the following alternate flavorings and colorings to create Delights from other planets that are simply out of this world!

Crème de cassis with dark pink coloring
Curacao with blue coloring
Crème de violette with purple coloring
Peach schnapps with orange coloring
Apricot brandy with yellow coloring

Ingredients

FOR THE DELIGHT

225g (8 oz.) white granulated sugar

70ml (2½ fl. oz.) water (for first mixture)

55g (2 oz.) corn flour

100g (3½ oz.) icing sugar

300ml (½ pt.) water (for second mixture)

1.25 ml (¼ tsp.) cream of tartar

30ml (2 tbsp.) absinthe

5ml (1 tsp.) liquid glucose, corn syrup or golden syrup

Green food coloring

FOR DUSTING MIX

15g (½ oz.) corn flour

15g (½ oz.) icing sugar

6 Add the cream of tartar and continue to heat and stir frequently over a low flame for 20–30 minutes. Your mixture should be very thick, hard to stir and pale lemon yellow in color.

7 Remove from the heat and beat in the liquid glucose and absinthe. Add a couple of drops of food coloring to give the mixture a green hue.

8 Pour the mixture into the lined tin and leave overnight to set.

To Finish

1 Remove from tin and cut into squares. Toss in the dusting mix and allow to dry a few hours before putting in airtight boxes with more of the dusting mix.

PANTRY PERFECTIONS

It is important to make sure the mixture is very thick before adding the absinthe and glucose, as these will soften it again. If it has been insufficiently cooked, it will be reluctant to set, resulting in a gooey paste rather than a nice slab that can be cut into squares.

These sweets will keep well for a week or two in a single layer; though, the longer they are kept, the harder the outer sugary crust will become and the softer the inside will get.

Chocolate Elegance Scones

Inside the casino on level nine, the cards were being dealt and the chips gathered in. Gentlemen clustered in groups, their smart evening dress exquisitely pressed, while the occasional lady in bright silks hovered like an exotic bird in a group of corvids.

At a small table in a darkened corner, Ace Blincoe stared at his opponent, heir to the largest cake empire on earth, Herbert Cholmondey, drink in hand. Each onlooker held his breath as the dealer turned the final card. A gasp rippled around the room. Ace smiled.

So it was that Ace walked away from the table with the secret recipe for Cholmondey's chocolate scones safely tucked into his waistcoat pocket and an entire empire of patisserie at his beck and call. Blincoe's Buns were to become legendary throughout four galaxies and a staple of the Mauve Star Liner's breakfasts.

Ingredients

55g (2 oz.) chopped dates

5g (1 tsp.) bicarbonate of soda (baking soda)

60ml (2 fl. oz.) boiling water

140g (5 oz.) gluten-free self-rising flour

15g (½ oz.) cocoa powder

45g (1½ oz.) butter

55g (2 oz.) chocolate, chopped, or small
covertures chocolate drops

55g (2 oz.) dark brown sugar

40 ml (1½ fl. oz.) milk

1 egg, beaten

Sifted icing sugar

*Makes 8 scones

1 Preheat the oven to gas mark 6 (400° F/200° C). Place the dates, bicarbonate of soda and boiling water in a bowl. Allow the dates to soak for 30 minutes so they can absorb the water and get sticky.

2 Meanwhile, in a large bowl, mix the gluten-free flour and cocoa powder together.

3 Cut the butter into pieces and rub into the flour mix until it resembles fine bread crumbs. Then, stir in the sugar and finely chopped chocolate.

4 Make a well in the center of the dry mix and add the date mixture, milk and beaten egg. Fold the ingredients into the dry mixture with a large metal spoon until combined. Leave to rest for 5 minutes.

5 On a very well floured baking tray, pat the mixture into a square with floured hands, then cut into 8 rectangles. Bake for 10–12 minutes.

6 Cool the scones on the baking tray for 1 minute, then transfer to a wire rack.

7 Once cooled, dust liberally with sifted icing sugar.

PANTRY PERFECTIONS

I like to use gluten-free flour for these scones, as it yields a crumblier texture. You can use a normal self-rising flour if you prefer; just keep in mind that your scones will be slightly springier.

PANTRY PERFECTIONS

Because these scones are a very sophisticated dark chocolate base and not a sweet brownie-like cake, they should be served with butter, jam and cream. Hazelnut chocolate spread and cream is another delightful topping option.

While they really are best eaten warm from the oven, they can be eaten cold within a day or two if stored properly in an airtight container. They will also keep well in the freezer for up to a month if stored on the day they are made. Simply defrost, warm in the oven for a few minutes and enjoy!

HOUSEKEEPER'S PERKS

For a delicious batch of chocolate orange scones, simply add 15g (1 tsp.) of orange zest to the flour mix and substitute orange juice for the milk. Serve with marmalade instead of jam.

For white chocolate and banana scones, substitute white chocolate powder for the cocoa powder and use white sugar in place of dark brown sugar. Use 60g (2 oz.) of chopped banana in place of the dates and replace the dark chopped chocolate with white chocolate. Most white chocolate powders have sugar in them, resulting in a sweeter, lighter scone. As such, it can be served with just butter or cream.

Gin and Tonic Cake

The grand vista of the busy departure lounge spreads before Lord and Lady Montmorency-Skye. Dozens of smartly dressed porters scurried hither and thither, their blue and gold uniforms bright among the crowds. Towering stacks of steamer trunks and elegant portmanteaus were whisked out of sight on automated brass and mahogany carriages.

The tea rooms on the first floor are a perfect place to watch the activity and see the people who are about to embark on their Grand Tour. While sipping Darjeeling and eating the exquisite cake of La Petite Choux, Lady Montmorency-Skye spotted a prima ballerina, an eloping couple, the millionaire playboy genius Antonius Starke and a notorious jewel thief in disguise.

Ingredients

FOR THE CAKE

24 rose geranium leaves (optional)

200g (7 oz.) white fat or shortening (such as Trex or Cookeen)

315g (11 oz.) white caster sugar

5ml (1 tsp.) vanilla essence

5ml (1 tsp.) rose essence (optional)

450g (1 lb.) plain flour

1.25g (¼ tsp.) salt

20g (4 tsp.) baking powder

320 ml (11 fl. oz.) milk

4 egg whites

FOR THE JAM

1 cucumber, finely grated

Juice of ½ lemon

Jam sugar (sugar with added pectin) equal in weight to grated cucumber

FOR THE CREAM

1.2L (2 pt.) double cream

30ml (2 tbsp.) Hendrick's gin

FOR DECORATION

Edible silver stars and sequins

Special Supplies

Jam jars with lids

Wax disks

*Makes 12 tall slices

TO MAKE THE CAKE

1 Preheat the oven to gas mark 4 (350° F/180° C). Line and grease 6 shallow 7" (18cm) cake tins. If using the rose geranium leaves, place 4 leaves flat on the base of each pan.

2 Cream the fat and 200g (7 oz.) of the sugar together until light and fluffy. Add the vanilla and rose essence and blend thoroughly.

3 In a separate bowl, mix together the flour, salt and baking powder. Add this mixture to the creamed fat and sugar a spoonful at a time, alternating with the milk.

4 In another large bowl, whisk the egg whites until stiff. Fold in the remaining sugar until thoroughly mixed. Be careful not to overmix, or the egg whites will lose their shape.

5 Pour the batter into the egg mix, folding gently with a metal spoon. Again, don't overmix; it should be fully blended but still light and airy.

6 Working quickly, divide the mixture into 2 bowls. From the first bowl, place a third of the mixture in one tin. Then, add 3 drops of coloring to the remaining mix. Blend gently and spoon half the colored mix into another tin. Add 3 more drops of color to the remaining mix, then spoon into a third tin.

7 Add 9 drops of color to the second bowl and blend well. Place a third of the mixture in one tin. Add 3 additional drops of color to the mix and place another third in a second tin. Finally, add 3 drops of color to the last of the mixture and spoon into a third tin. All 6 tins should now be full of mixtures varying in color.

8 Bake all the cakes for 10–15 minutes or until a skewer comes out clean. Try not to let them get golden around the edges or you will lose the perfect color effect.

9 Cool each layer in its tin for 30 minutes, then gently turn out on a wire rack. When completely cool, peel away the lining paper and geranium leaves.

FOR THE CUCUMBER JAM

1 Grate 1 cucumber. Weigh this, then place into a large pan with lemon juice. Add the equivalent weight in jam sugar, heating slowly until the sugar has dissolved. Boil rapidly for approximately 4 minutes, or as directed on the sugar packet.

2 Pour the jam into sterilized jars. Top each jar with a wax disk and allow to cool. Once cool, add an airtight lid and store in the fridge until needed.

PANTRY PERFECTIONS

This recipe was designed to highlight the unusual cucumber and rose notes of Hendrick's gin. Other gins have different flavor notes, so choose cake flavors that complement your gin. For example, pair a gin with citrus notes with orange curd and 5g (1 tsp.) of orange zest added to the cake mix.

Many small batch gins have their own mix of extra botanicals which impart distinctive flavors, such as cinnamon, lime or even lavender. If you research which unique notes are present in your gin, then you can enhance them by choosing complementary flavors for your cake and jam.

For the Cream

1 Whisk the cream until very stiff, then whisk in the gin, spoon by spoon. Don't over whisk or it will not remain firm. Likewise, don't be tempted to add more gin, or the cream will go runny.

To Assemble the Cake

1 Place the darkest color sponge on a cake board. Sprinkle the top with gin (a little plant mister filled with alcohol works beautifully for this), then spread a liberal amount of cucumber jam, followed by gin cream. Add the next, slightly lighter colored layer of sponge. Sprinkle with gin and add jam and cream as before. Repeat until all the layers have been used up, making sure each layer is stable and correctly placed before moving on to the next.

2 Cover the top and sides of the cake with the remaining whipped cream. Decorate with plenty of edible silver stars and sequins.

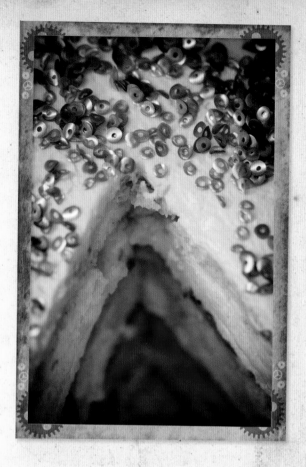

HOUSEKEEPER'S PERKS

A cocktail is always a delightful addition to an afternoon tea, but rather than the conventional champagne, why not try a Steamer B? To make this delightful concoction, you will need 1 measure of Hendrick's gin and 3 measures of strongly brewed blackberry and apple fruit tea that has been allowed to cool.

Shake together thoroughly over ice (you could add a tiny drop of honey if you have a sweet tooth). Serve in a teacup with a slice of apple instead of a biscuit.

The Steamer B can also be served warm as a heartening brew. Just add the gin to the warm tea.

PANTRY PERFECTIONS

This is a truly epic cake suitable for a large party or special occasion. You can easily half the quantities to create a three-layer cake of equal deliciousness. Halving the amounts also gives you sufficient quantity for 12 cupcakes if you prefer an individual portion. Just swirl two colors of the mixture into cupcake cases, omitting the geranium leaves. Bake for only 10 minutes and cool in their cases on a wire rack before spreading with the cucumber jam and piping a swirl of the gin cream on the top.

AIRSHIP CAKE POPS

"Why, Miss Amber, Miss Scarlett, are you not ready yet?! They have been waiting for you in the Dining Room for ten minutes!" The gleaming brass and mahogany mechanical governess floated around the room, gathering dresses and hair ribbons before starting to thrust the reluctant girls into frills and pinafores.

"When I grow up, I shall be the captain of a ship just like this one, and we shall sail to the furthest galaxy," Miss Amber said, turning her shining eyes on the governess. "And I will have a pirate ship like Andromeda Darkstorm so we can play chase," the other little girl announced. "Well, no one is going to have a thing but bread and water for tea if you don't hurry up!" the governess said sternly as, far overhead, the rings of Saturn twinkled like fairy dust.

Ingredients

FOR THE CAKE

55g (2 oz.) crunchy or smooth peanut butter

55g (2 oz.) flour

55g (2 oz.) sugar

1 egg

15ml (1 tbsp.) oil

30ml (2 tbsp.) milk

FOR THE ICING

30g (1 oz.) icing sugar

30g (1 oz.) butter

30g (1 oz.) melted chocolate, allowed
to cool a little

FOR DECORATION

Bag of candy melts

Decorations like silver and gold balls,
chocolate buttons, modeled pieces, etc.

Special Supplies

Parchment paper

8 sticks (one for each pop)

Tall glasses (to hold the cake pops while
decorating)

Knife with ridged edge

Chopsticks

* Makes 8 large cake pops

To Make the Cake Pop Mixture

1 Preheat the oven to gas mark 6 (400° F/200° C. Line a small loaf tin with parchment paper.

2 Rub the peanut butter into the flour until it resembles bread crumbs, just as you would if using butter or margarine. Stir in the sugar.

3 Beat the egg, oil and milk together in a bowl, then stir into the flour mix.

4 Pour the batter into the loaf tin and bake for 15–20 minutes or until a skewer comes out clean.

5 Remove the cake from the tin, peel off the lining paper and cool on a wire rack.

6 While the cake is cooling, make some icing by creaming icing sugar and butter together. Pour in the melted chocolate and mix thoroughly.

7 In a large bowl, break the cooled cake into small pieces, crumbling it into a bread crumb texture.

8 Mix the icing into the bread crumb mixture until it resembles modeling dough.

PANTRY PERFECTIONS

If you aren't keen on peanut butter, you can use any flavor cake, even the off cuts or trimmings from a fancy-shaped cake. You don't have to make airships, either. The cake mix of 225g (8 oz.) sponge cake crumbs to 85g (3 oz.) of butter icing can be modeled into any basic shape, including top hats, air balloons or moustaches. Just add extra details once it's been covered with candy melt.

To Make the Airships

1 Divide the mixture into 8 chunks. (This makes large airships. You can divide further to make smaller ones if you like.)

2 Form a piece of the mixture into a ball by squeezing it between your hands and then slightly taper one end. Do this for all the pieces, placing them on a baking tray when done.

3 Melt some of the covering candy melts as directed on the package. Dip roughly half of a stick into the melted mixture, then immediately press the stick into a molded cake pop. Repeat for all the pops.

4 Place the pops into the fridge to firm up for about 30 minutes, then prepare your decorative touches (silver and gold balls, buttons cut in half to make tail fins or propellers, etc.).

5 Melt the remaining candy melts in a small, deep bowl. Spoon the melted mixture over each pop, allowing it to drip back into the bowl. Smooth with a knife to get the ridged balloon look.

6 While the covering is still wet, add decorations by pressing them into the melt with the point of a chopstick. Place each completed cake pop in a tall, heavy glass to set until firm.

7 Pipe additional decorations on the set pops with warm candy melts or royal icing.

PANTRY PERFECTIONS

Candy melts come in a wide variety of colors and even flavors. They are easier to work with than chocolate as they do not require tempering to maintain their color and sheen. They are also ideal for using in molds to make interesting steampunk shapes and designs, and can be dusted with edible metallic powders for a shiny tone. Why not try molding some extra pieces to add to the cake pop shapes when they are finished?

CHAPTER TWO

THE SCIENTIFIC CHATEAU

Dear Lord Byron,

Thank you so much for your introduction to Doctor Ruthven. Our balloon landed perfectly in a useful clearing, and though there were several rather large and ominous dogs roaming about, they soon ran off when our host appeared.

The Chateau is truly magnificent, with its oak panels and chandeliers everywhere, though much of it is taken over with laboratory equipment and unusual inventions of grand scale. As for our host, he really is rather splendid looking, though I'm not sure of his penchant for black leather; I can't help but think that something cheery in green or gold might brighten the place up a little.

Tonight, he has invited a few friends for cake and conversation. They are a gloriously intellectual group. Vicomte Guittet has been talking about his chemistry experiments with little demonstrations of Scientific Principles, Mrs. Shelley read aloud from her scientific romance, and Miss Lovelace has even offered to show me her calculations one evening!

I also have a tincture for you, compliments of the Doctor, though it is a rather nasty shade of orange and smells even worse. I wouldn't touch it if I were you. . . .

Love and admiration as always,
Emilly

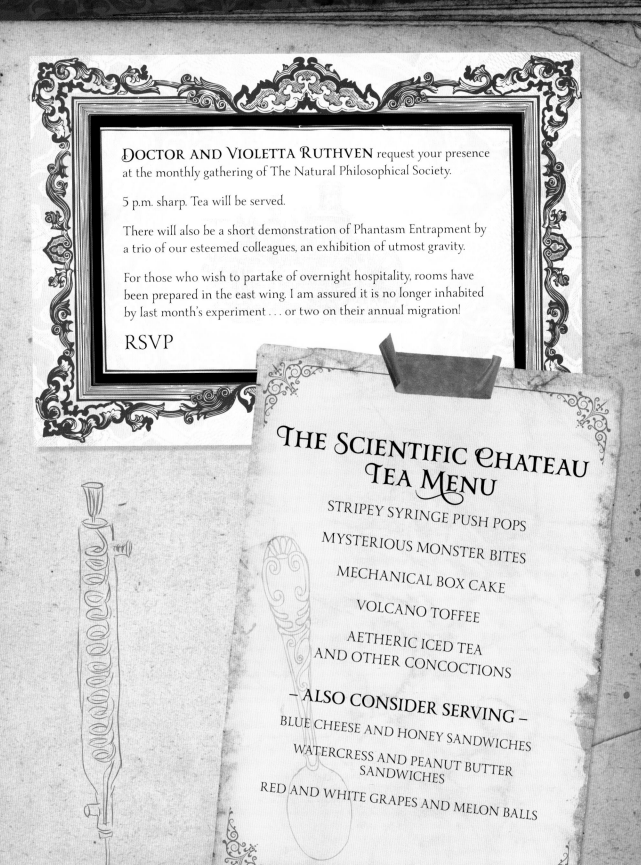

Doctor and Violetta Ruthven request your presence at the monthly gathering of The Natural Philosophical Society.

5 p.m. sharp. Tea will be served.

There will also be a short demonstration of Phantasm Entrapment by a trio of our esteemed colleagues, an exhibition of utmost gravity.

For those who wish to partake of overnight hospitality, rooms have been prepared in the east wing. I am assured it is no longer inhabited by last month's experiment . . . or two on their annual migration!

RSVP

The Scientific Chateau Tea Menu

STRIPEY SYRINGE PUSH POPS

MYSTERIOUS MONSTER BITES

MECHANICAL BOX CAKE

VOLCANO TOFFEE

AETHERIC ICED TEA
AND OTHER CONCOCTIONS

– ALSO CONSIDER SERVING –

BLUE CHEESE AND HONEY SANDWICHES

WATERCRESS AND PEANUT BUTTER
SANDWICHES

RED AND WHITE GRAPES AND MELON BALLS

STRIPEY SYRINGE PUSH POPS

A shadowy figure in an apron and cap walks the long corridor with a covered silver tray. Shrieks echo through the empty abbey, carried on the wind through the rafters. Thumps and crashes from the attic do not disturb her. Even though it sounds as if furniture is being hurled by a being with superhuman strength, she marches stoically on toward her destination. Finally, lifting an ancient tapestry, the nurse opens a hidden door and ascends the narrow staircase. Herr Doktor waits.

A shard of light shines upon the silver tray, now set down upon the floor. The door cracks open slowly, just enough for a cold white hand to reach out and grasp the cake....

Ingredients

FOR THE CAKE

115g (4 oz.) butter

115g (4 oz.) sugar

115g (4 oz.) self-rising flour

2 eggs

Deep red/pink food coloring

55g (2 oz.) grated white chocolate

85g (3 oz.) fresh or frozen raspberries
[or 30g (2 tbsp.) of whole fruit raspberry
jam]

FOR THE GANACHE

40g (1½ oz.) cream

100g (3½ oz.) white chocolate, roughly
chopped

FOR THE ICING

115g (4 oz.) butter

115g (4 oz.) icing sugar

Purple food coloring

5ml (1 tsp.) of vanilla extract

FOR DECORATION

Edible stars, glitter, sequins, colored sugar
or any other decoration you prefer

Special Supplies

6 pop cases

Piping bag with star nozzle

*Makes 6 push pops

TO MAKE THE CAKES

1 Preheat the oven to gas mark 5
(375° F/190° C) and grease and line 2
shallow 7" (18cm) round pans.

2 Using either a wooden spoon or an
electric mixer, cream the butter and
sugar together until light and fluffy.

3 Add the flour, eggs, food coloring
and chocolate, and mix until
smooth.

4 Gently stir in the raspberries so
they ripple through the mixture
rather than completely blending them
in.

5 Pour an equal amount of batter into
both of the tins. Bake for around 20
minutes or until the cakes spring back
when pressed in the center.

6 Remove from the tins and cool on a
wire rack.

HOUSEKEEPER'S PERKS

This cake and icing combination
also makes delectable cupcakes.
Mix up the cake batter following
steps 1–3. Place 12 paper cases in
a muffin tray and fill halfway,
using about ¾ of the cake mix.
Make a little well in the center of
each cake and place a teaspoon of
raspberries in it, covering all the
raspberries with the remaining
cake mix. Bake the cupcakes for
only 10–15 minutes, cool in their
cases on a wire rack, then ice and
decorate. When you bite into a
cake the raspberries will ooze out!

For the Ganache and Icing

1 To make the ganache, heat the cream until it reaches a boil. Add the chopped white chocolate to the boiling cream and mix until smooth. Leave to cool completely.

2 Make the butter icing by beating the butter and icing sugar together with the food coloring and vanilla.

3 Beat the ganache and butter icing together. Leave in the refrigerator for at least an hour to set.

PANTRY PERFECTIONS

To maintain the perfect presentation of the push pops, it is imperative to keep them cool. The truffle icing melts very quickly if it is allowed to become warm! They are best stored in a cool cupboard rather than a refrigerator and should be eaten within a day or two of assembling.

To Assemble the Pops

1 Cut out rounds of cake using a pop case.

2 Beat the icing until smooth and slightly softened. I use an electric whisk to get it to just the right consistency after it's been in the refrigerator overnight. Then, place a large star nozzle in a piping bag and fill with the icing.

3 Place a round of cake in each pop case, followed by a swirl of icing. Sprinkle edible stars, glitter, sequins, colored sugar chips, etc. down the sides.

4 Add another round of cake, followed by another swirl and more decorations. Then, place a third piece of cake and a final icing swirl, decorating with your chosen sprinkles.

MYSTERIOUS
MONSTER BITES

In the silence of Doctor Ruthven's library at midnight, the dusty cabinets stand tall, filled with fancies from all four corners of the earth. Giant eggs of the fabled Roc; wax seals of long-dead emperors; tablets inscribed with unknowable letters—these are but a few of the many mysterious treasures that abound. Surely, if one could just unlock the secrets of an ancient scroll or two, the wonders of the universe would open, bringing enlightenment, peace and fame to the bearer of the news.

So it is that Lady Armstrong Prior sits night after night, candle wax dripping on the mahogany desk and quill in hand, desperately unraveling the codex that will divulge the secret recipe for Cleopatra's favorite snack.

Ingredients

175g (6 oz.) butter

Finely grated peel of an orange

Finely grated peel of a lime

Green and orange food coloring (optional)

350g (12 oz.) flour

55g (2 oz.) ground almonds

220g (7 oz.) caster sugar

2 eggs

*Makes 12 biscuits

To Make the Biscuits

1 Beat the butter until soft. Divide into 2 equal portions and add the lime peel to one and the orange peel to the other. You can also add a few drops of food coloring at this stage.

2 Mix the flour, ground almonds and sugar thoroughly in a separate bowl. Divide the dry mix in half and add each of the portions to the separate bowls of flavored butter.

3 Add an egg to each bowlful and gently stir with a wooden spoon until all the ingredients are thoroughly combined.

4 Roll each mixture into a long sausage shape on a floured board, about 12" (30cm) should do. Twist the two flavored lengths together, striping the mixture so it looks a little like a candy cane. Roll gently to merge the edges and cut into two equal lengths. Refrigerate the dough for an hour to allow the mixture to firm up again.

HOUSEKEEPER'S PERKS

For a richer treat, try chocolate orange biscuits. All you need to do is replace the lime peel and juice with one dessert spoon of cocoa powder mixed into half of the flour mix.
For a refreshing citrus variation, try lemon lime biscuits. Simply replace the orange peel and juice with lemon peel and juice.

5 Sprinkle your work surface with flour and roll out the first dough piece to about ¼" (6mm) thickness. Cut out your monsters or dinosaurs, trying to get a bit of each color on each biscuit and being as economic as possible with leftover dough. Repeat with the other dough piece.

6 Preheat the oven to gas mark 4 (350° F/180° C). Use any leftover dough to make rocks and boulders for the dinosaurs to rampage through, or press together and re-roll.

7 Place the monsters on a lightly oiled baking tray with a 1" (2.5cm) or so between them and bake for around 10 minutes. Remove from the oven and cool the biscuits on a wire rack.

SCULLERY STORIES

Biscuits are one of the most popular foodstuffs to take on an expedition. They don't take up much space, and they provide plenty of carbohydrates for energy. The name comes from the Latin *bis coquere* meaning "cooked twice." Adventurers and sailors noticed that biscuits softened with age, so in order to maintain crispness on long voyages, hardtack was baked up to four times.

Mechanical Box Cake

Gilded carriages drawn by dark plumed horses arrived one by one, depositing masked revelers cloaked in silk and velvet onto the moonlit steps. It is the Count Von Rottenberg's birthday, and he has an amazing new device to demonstrate in the cellar of Dr. Ruthven's Chateau. As guests descend into the gloomy depths, Von Rottenberg's whirring mahogany and brass device can be seen gleaming through the darkness with a strange glow. The guests cluster around begging for a look, as he ushers them into the chamber of the machine, never again to be seen; although, the Count's troupe of performing monkeys are now legendary across Europe.

Ingredients

FOR THE ALMOND CAKE

115g (4 oz.) butter

115g (4 oz.) sugar

115g (4 oz.) self-rising flour

2 eggs

30 ml (1 fl. oz.) amaretto [or 30ml (1 fl. oz.) milk and a few drops almond essence]

FOR THE CHOCOLATE CAKE

30 ml (1 fl. oz.) milk

115g (4 oz.) chocolate, chopped

115g (4 oz.) butter

115g (4 oz.) sugar

2 eggs

115g (4 oz.) self-rising flour

FOR THE BUTTER ICING

115g (4 oz.) butter

115g (4 oz.) icing sugar

5ml (1 tsp.) vanilla extract

FOR THE MARZIPAN COVERING

400g (14 oz.) ready made marzipan

20g ($^3/_4$ oz.) cocoa powder

FOR THE GANACHE

100g (3$^1/_2$ oz.) cream

200g (7 oz.) dark chocolate, chopped

FOR DECORATION

Some cogs and gear wheels scrubbed clean in boiling water and dried thoroughly

2 part food-grade silicone molding putty

Brown flower petal paste and chocolate ready-to-roll icing

Edible metallic powders

Special Supplies

Serrated bread knife

TO MAKE THE ALMOND CAKE

1 Preheat the oven to gas mark 6 (400° F/200° C) and grease and line a 6" (15cm) square tin.

2 Cream the butter and sugar together until light and fluffy. Add the flour, eggs and amaretto, and mix until smooth.

3 Pour the batter into the prepared tin and bake for 30–35 minutes, or until the cake springs back when pressed in the center. Remove from tin and cool on a wire rack.

TO MAKE THE CHOCOLATE CAKE

1 Heat the milk in the microwave or a small pan until it reaches a boil. Add the chopped chocolate and stir until completely melted.

2 Cream the butter and sugar together as before, then add all remaining ingredients, including the chocolate mixture. Mix until smooth.

3 Re-grease and line the 6" (15cm) tin and bake as directed for the almond cake.

To Assemble the Cake

1 Make butter icing by beating butter, icing sugar and vanilla together until light and fluffy.

2 Roll out the marzipan and sprinkle cocoa on top. Roll up like a jelly roll. On a board lightly dusted with icing sugar, knead until thoroughly combined.

3 Trim the tops of both cakes with a large serrated bread knife. Make sure both cake tops are perfectly level; this will help with the assembling.

4 Place one cake on top of the other and trim all 4 sides, removing any hard crust edges. Then slice down through both cakes, cutting them into 4 strips. Swap 2 strips of each color, top to bottom, creating a chessboard design.

5 Remove the top cake. Glue each strip of the bottom cake to its neighbour using butter icing. You don't need loads of icing, but make sure you go to the edges. Scrape off the excess. Attach all 4 strips together neatly and add a thicker layer of butter icing all over the top.

6 Glue the top cake strips together with butter icing in the same way and place on top of the bottom cake, maintaining the chess board design. Gently press so all pieces are firmly attached and the cake is nice and square. Place a covering of butter icing over the top and sides, scraping most off as before. This will act as glue for the marzipan. Place the cake on an 8" (20cm) cake board.

To Ice the Cake

1 On a board dusted with icing sugar, roll out the marzipan to around ¼" (6mm) thickness. Place over the cake and lightly stroke and smooth all over until it covers the cake and board perfectly (see YouTube video for a demonstration). Trim around the edges.

2 Make ganache by heating the cream until it reaches a boil. Remove from heat and mix in the chopped chocolate. Beat with a wooden spoon until all the chocolate is melted and turns thick and shiny. Leave to cool for about an hour. When cool, pour over the cake, coating it completely. Leave to set.

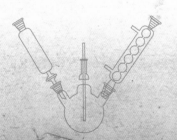

To Make the Chocolate Cogs and Decoration

1 Mix equal amounts of each part of the food-grade silicone molding putty and knead thoroughly until it is all one color. Form into a shape that is twice as deep and slightly larger in surface area than the object you want to mold.

2 Take your item and press it face down into the molding putty. Try not to wriggle it as you press, or you may distort the shape. Leave to set for about an hour, then remove the original item.

3 Create a mixture of half sugar flower petal paste and half ready-to-roll chocolate icing to get a firm modeling dough. Press it into the mold, making sure to fill all the little crevices. Use a sharp knife to trim any excess and ease from the mold.

4 Using your finger and a small amount of edible metallic powder, gently rub color over the raised areas. You can add subsequent coats if necessary, but only rub on a little at a time. This will keep the recessed areas dark and prevent loose powder from floating about.

5 To attach the cogs, press them into the not-quite-set ganache. If the ganache is too runny, they will simply slide down, so wait half an hour or so before placing the cogs. If it has set too much, just melt leftover ganache in a little bowl, paint it on the back of the cogs and use it like glue.

44

PANTRY PERFECTIONS

If you don't want to use the molded cogs immediately, they can be kept in an airtight container for up to a month. They make wonderful additions to cupcakes, too.

You don't have to use chocolate-flavored icing either; why not try lemon for lemon cupcakes or white chocolate for vanilla ones? Just use a molded base that is the same color as your main icing so it will blend in when you place them on your cakes.

VOLCANO TOFFEE

When the Society of Investigative Natural Philosophers takes it in turns to host their monthly lecture, they love to impress the other members with a showy dinner, perhaps with fireworks or a display of scientific principles afterwards. Lord Francis Rockett was feted in the society annals when he combined the two in his marvelous tabletop volcano toffee dispenser. In the darkened hall, amid a fog of dry ice, the volcano overflowed, creating rivers of edible molten lava!

Poor cook was at a total loss as what to do with all the left over toffee, and the servants ate nothing else for weeks. This is a far more sensible method and quantity....

Ingredients

15g (1 heaping tsp.) bicarbonate of soda (baking soda)

45ml (3 tbsp.) golden syrup (or corn syrup)

15ml (1 tbsp.) cider vinegar (or malt or white wine vinegar)

Juice of $\frac{1}{2}$ lemon

75g ($2\frac{3}{4}$ oz.) light brown sugar

75g ($2\frac{3}{4}$ oz.) white sugar

200g (7oz.) dark chocolate for coating

100g ($3\frac{1}{2}$ oz.) red/strawberry chocolate melt (optional)

Red edible glitter flakes (optional)

1 Grease a piece of baking paper with butter or margarine and use it to line a 7" (18cm) square tin.

2 Fill a bowl with ice cubes and nestle the lined baking tray inside of it, being careful not to get the baking paper wet. Make sure there is a layer of ice under the tray as well as around the sides.

3 Measure out the bicarbonate of soda and put to one side.

4 In a very large pan on low heat, gently stir the golden syrup, vinegar and lemon juice together using a wooden spoon. Continue to stir until the mixture reaches a syrup-like consistency.

5 Add both sugars and stir until dissolved. Try not to get any on the sides of the pan where it will burn. When the sugar is completely dissolved, stop stirring, turn up the heat and boil hard for 3 minutes. Turn off the heat.

6 Immediately add the bicarbonate of soda and mix quickly but thoroughly as the toffee bubbles up like a volcano. Do not overmix or it will deflate and become soggy. Be very careful: This mixture is boiling hot!

7 Very quickly, while it is still aerated and bubbling, pour the mixture into the cold tin and leave to set in the ice cube bath.

PANTRY PERFECTIONS

When bicarbonate of soda is added to vinegar an extraordinary chemical reaction occurs. This reaction is responsible for creating the honeycomb air pockets in the toffee. If it doesn't fluff up, it may be because your bicarbonate is too old.

To maintain maximum fluffiness, it's best to cool the toffee very quickly, hence the tin in the ice bath. If it goes flat and loses its honeycomb-like appearance, it was not cooled quickly enough.

8 When thoroughly set, break into bite-sized pieces and set to the side. Melt chocolate by placing chopped pieces in a microwave-proof bowl and heating for 30 seconds. Stir and repeat if necessary, being careful not to overheat the chocolate.

9 Dip the broken toffee pieces in the melted chocolate. Cover each piece completely and leave to set on a baking tray.

10 Once the first layer is set, dip the ends in red chocolate melt and dust with glitter to give the impression of hot rock lava.

HOUSEKEEPER'S PERKS

Dipping the toffee in chocolate adds flavor as well as protects it. If you don't cover it in chocolate, it will quickly become sticky due to prolonged exposure to the air.

Try adorning your toffee with different flavors of chocolate for an extra dimensional thrill; some of Dr. Ruthven's favorites include the following:

dark chocolate with a pinch of chili flakes for an added layer of sophistication;

orange chocolate with a piece of gold leaf decoration for a decadent presentation;

unusual flavored candy melts combined with chocolate for a scrumptious surprise.

AETHERIC ICED TEA AND OTHER CONCOCTIONS

Deep within the laboratory something is brewing! Flasks bubble and hiss, and guests are under strict orders not to touch anything! Despite being shunned by society for his bizarre experiments, Doctor Ruthven's laboratory is a wonderland of extraordinary potions and lotions. He has been long under the surveillance of several freelance monster hunters, whose suspicions were aroused by rumours of peculiar creatures that emerge at dead of night, running into the surrounding forests at full moon. Investigation has so far only revealed a particularly friendly puppy ... that glows in the dark.

Ingredients

Per serving:

40ml (1½ oz.) vodka

20ml (¾ oz.) gin

20ml (¾ oz.) light tequila

20ml (¾ oz.) light rum

10ml (¼ oz.) white crème de menthe

40ml (1½ oz.) lemon and lime juice mixed

10ml (¼ oz.) sugar syrup

Cola

Edible gold glitter

To Make the Aetheric Iced Tea

1 Place a good handful of ice cubes in a shaker; add all the spirits, the juice and the syrup. Shake vigorously till a frost forms.

2 Fill a glass with ice cubes. Pour the contents of the shaker over the ice and top up with cola.

3 Sprinkle edible gold glitter over the drink to serve.

SCULLERY STORIES

The reason this delightful drink is called a tea is all due to prohibition. In order to avoid arrest and imprisonment or heavy fines during the alcohol ban, this mixture—which is, after all, colored a little like tea—was drunk from cups and saucers to try and fool the cops. Even now, I must admit I have always had my suspicions about a few tea-drinking aunts who insist on lemon, not milk. . . .

DNA DAIQUIRI

Per serving:
50g (1¾ oz.) strawberries (frozen)
30ml (1 oz.) white rum (1 UK shot)
30ml (1 oz.) fresh pineapple juice
Lime juice
Icing sugar

- *Chill the rum in the freezer for at least 2 hours.*
- *Dip the rim of the glass (a martini glass looks nice) in the lime juice, then the icing sugar.*
- *Pour in the cold rum. Blend strawberries with the pineapple juice very briefly (a 10-second whiz should do it).*
- *Very carefully, add the strawberry puree to the top of the rum.*

THE GREEN FAIRY

Per serving:
50ml (1½ oz.) absinthe
100ml (3½ oz.) ice cold cream soda

- *Pour the absinthe into the glass and slowly drip in the ice-cold cream soda. Watch the green fairy turn the clear green absinthe cloudy white.*

THE SECRETS BEHIND THE DNA DAIQUIRI

Every living cell has DNA in it, but sometimes it's a bit tricky to get it out. Strawberries (or any other soft, pulpy fruit like kiwi or melon) make the job a bit easier. Freezing them destroys their cell membranes, which is why they go to mush when you defrost them. It also, quite handily, releases their DNA from the nucleus. The pineapple juice contains enzymes that break down the proteins found in the cell and cleans the DNA up; but if you leave the mixture for too long, the pineapple juice will start to destroy the DNA as well, so don't hang about!

THE SECRETS BEHIND THE GREEN FAIRY

Louching is the term given to the magical effect of cream soda on absinthe. The particulates in the absinthe with bad solubility (anethol from anise, fennel and star anise) are released from the alcohol, creating a suspension of fine particles clouding the drink. A beautiful opal white bloom appears, spreading slowly through the glass as more cream soda is added, leading to the myth of the magical green fairy.

GENTLEMAN'S STUDY

Per serving:
20ml (³/₄oz.) Kahlua
20ml (³/₄oz.) Galliano
10ml (¹/₄oz.) Baileys Irish Cream
10ml (¹/₄oz.) single (light) cream

· *Chill all the ingredients well in the refrigerator or freezer.*
· *Mix the Baileys and cream together in a small glass.*
· *Carefully pour the Kahlua into the bottom of the glass. Pour the Galliano on top, trickling it down the side of the glass or over a bar spoon. Float the Baileys and cream mixture on the top.*
· *Serve with coffee and cigars in the study.*

GLOW AND TONIC

Per serving:
40ml (1¹/₂ oz.) gin
10ml (¹/₄oz.) Cointreau
150ml (5¹/₂ oz.) tonic water
Ice
Garnish (lemon, lime, orange, cucumber etc.)

· *Shake the Cointreau and gin together in a shaker with lots of ice.*
· *Pour into a glass and top up with tonic water.*
· *Garnish as appropriate to your preferred brand of gin.*
· *Serve near a UV light.*

THE SECRETS BEHIND THE GENTLEMAN'S STUDY

There is a science behind creating a layered drink like the Gentleman's Study. Every liquid has its own specific gravity. By discovering the gravity for a series of liquids, it is easy to determine which of them will sink and will need to be layered at the bottom of the glass and which will float to the top! The greater the differences in gravities, the less likely the two liquids are to mix and will instead create nice, clean layers. Chilling the alcohol thoroughly also helps with this.

THE SECRETS BEHIND THE GLOW AND TONIC

What gives a Glow and Tonic its lovely blue hue? It's the quinine contained in the tonic water. Quinine is manufactured from the bark of the Cinchona tree, which originates in Peru. The Cinchona tree has assorted medicinal properties, the most well known being its antimalarial powers, which were known as early as 1631. Missionaries first brought the medicine back from Peru to Europe, leading to its nickname "Jesuit's bark." When in mosquito-ridden warmer climes, colonial Victorians would mix the bitter medicine with gin to disguise the taste, and so the gin and tonic was born.

STRIPEY STOCKING

Per serving:
10ml (¼ oz.) EIC poppy syrup
10ml (¼ oz.) Fruiss Violet Syrup
15ml (½ oz.) De Kuyper Blue Curaco
15ml (½ oz.) Orchards Peach Schnapps
20ml (¾ oz.) Eristoff Black Vodka
20ml (¾ oz.) Absolut Raspberri vodka

· *Chill all the liqueurs thoroughly.*
· *Starting with the syrup, slowly pour each layer in turn over a bar spoon or down the side of the glass.*
· *Serve with a wink.*

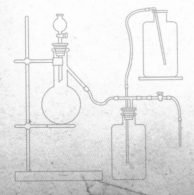

THE SECRETS BEHIND THE STRIPEY STOCKING

When making a layered drink like the Stripey Stocking, it's worth noting that different brands of the same spirit will sometimes have different specific gravities, so if something isn't working, that could well be why! A great deal depends on the percentage of alcohol. As a rough rule of thumb, the higher the alcohol content, the higher it'll be on the list.

This is a list of some of the most popular and colorful ingredients in gravity order, with the densest at the bottom of the list:

Gin (Tanqueray) 0.94
Tequila (Jose Cuervo) 0.95
Southern Comfort 0.97
Raspberry vodka (Smirnoff) 0.97
Double Cream 0.99
Chartreuse 0.99
Water 1.00
Jagermeister 1.01
Cinnamon schnapps (Goldslagger) 1.03
Cranberry juice 1.03
Orange juice 1.04
Malibu Rum 1.04
Cointreau 1.04
Benedictine 1.04
Apricot brandy (De Kuyper) 1.04
Apple juice 1.05
Limoncello 1.05
Bailey's Irish Cream 1.06
Blue curacao (De Kuyper) 1.07
Cherry brandy (Bols) 1.07
Green crème de menthe (De Kuyper) 1.08
Galliano 1.07
Amaretto (Disaronno) 1.08
Tia Maria 1.10
Midori Melon 1.11
White crème de menthe (De Kuyper) 1.11
Dark crème de cacao (De Kuyper) 1.11
White crème de cacao (De Kuyper) 1.12
Parfait amour (Bols) 1.12
Crème de cassis (De Kuyper) 1.12
Kahlua 1.14
Anisette 1.18
Grenadine (De Kuyper) 1.31

W. Gögler

BREGENZ.

54

CHAPTER THREE
A CURIOUS PICNIC

Darling Harry,

We had such a smashing picnic and met a multitude of your friends last Tuesday. Mr. Woppit introduced them all, but I'm afraid I got quite lost after the first ten or so. The balloon, however, was nearly lost after someone naughty nibbled through the rope and it started to sail off!

The mansion grounds are absolutely lovely, and the weather was splendid; parasols were most definitely needed. We had a lovely wander through the maze, although we never did seem to find the center. I carefully laid a trail of jelly beans to mark our path, as there seemed to be a magnet disruptor beam rendering the compass useless. Unfortunately, I think someone naughty must have been eating them as fast as I laid them down.

After tea, we had a game of cards and were shown a selection of amazing magic tricks. I'm fairly sure the magical disappearance and reappearance of several winning cards at opportune moments were purely coincidental and not an attempt to cheat by someone naughty!

We ate all the truffles, I'm afraid, but I saved you some coriander from the sandwiches.

All my Love,
Emilly

MR. WOPPIT cordially invites you to join him and his friends for a picnic tea in the garden.

3:30 p.m. or thereabouts, depending on the prevailing wind.

There is ample space for tethering your airship or balloon on the south lawn, and party games and croquet will be played for an assortment of delightful prizes throughout the afternoon. Do feel free to bring your own tablecloth and cushions.

Practical clothing is suggested, though waistcoats and bowties are optional.

RSVP

Curious Picnic Tea Menu

GINGERBREAD WOPPITS

STRAWBERRY AND ROSE CONSERVE

TEA TIME TRUFFLES

TIPSY TURVEY TEA BREAD

MAGICAL FRUIT SCONES

PADDINGTON COCKTAILS

– ALSO CONSIDER SERVING –

CHEESE STRAWS

CORIANDER, CHOPPED HAZELNUT AND CREAM CHEESE SANDWICHES

BANANA AND BROWN SUGAR SANDWICHES

JELLY BEANS

DARJEELING OR FRUIT TEA

GINGERBREAD WOPPITS

When entering a garden maze, it is always advisable to keep some biscuits upon one's person; one never knows just how long it may take to find the center and, afterwards, the egress.

Lady Jessica Shaw-Morton, adventurer and lady of fashion, swears by them as a restorative from the fatigues of exploration. Camping overnight in the very center of Hampton Court's yew lined puzzle, she once fended off a whole flock of racing pigeons with just one small biscuit from Fortnum and Masons. Quite how this was achieved depends rather on whom you ask; suggestions vary from throwing it as far as possible and shouting "fetch," to bribing a fellow maze explorer and dashing linguist to tell them politely that racing season was over.

Projectile or tea dueling component, these delightful fancies are sure to find a welcome place on any tea table, at home or, indeed, abroad.

Ingredients

FOR THE BISCUITS

225g (8 oz.) plain flour

5g (1 tsp.) ginger

5g (1 tsp.) cinnamon

115g (4 oz.) butter or margarine

115g (4 oz.) soft dark brown sugar

30ml (2 tbsp.) black treacle (blackstrap molasses)

30ml (2 tbsp.) golden syrup

FOR THE ICING

Icing sugar to coat your board

Small packet of colored ready-to-roll icing or rolled fondant

White fat or shortening

Gold, bronze or silver edible dust powder

Special Supplies

Cling film (plastic wrap)

Rubber stamps

*Makes 10–12 biscuits

TO MAKE THE CAKES

1 Preheat the oven to gas mark 4 (350° F/ 180° C). Sift the flour and spices together in a large bowl.

2 Cut the butter into small cubes and add to flour, mixing in all the other ingredients.

3 Knead lightly with a fork or your fingers until everything is fully blended. Wrap in cling film and place the dough in the refrigerator for at least an hour to firm up again. It will keep nicely overnight as well.

4 On a well floured board, carefully roll the dough out to about ¼" (6mm) thickness. The mixture will be quite sticky, so be gentle. Refrain from over flouring as well, or the biscuits will become tough.

5 Cut out bunnies, teapots or rocket shapes. Carefully lift the cutouts with a large palette knife and place on an oiled baking tray. For a soft style ginger cookie, bake for 10 minutes. If you like a crisper biscuit, bake for a little longer, roughly 15–18 minutes, keeping a careful eye on them so they don't burn.

6 Cool the biscuits on the tray for 5 minutes to firm up, then place them on a wire rack to cool completely.

SCULLERY STORIES

Early adventurers often found their exploits funded by wealthy patrons who desired spices from foreign lands. Ginger had a mysterious allure, and many tall tales were told in medieval times about its origins. One thirteenth-century French courtier thought it was fished from the Nile using nets, along with rhubarb, cinnamon and aloes! These exotic things from the Far East made lengthy journeys from countries such as India and China, passing through many hands for many months as trade caravans wound their way across the world. How much simpler things have become with the advent of fast ships, railways and aeronautics!

To Make the Fondant Icing

1 Lightly coat a board with icing sugar, then roll out the fondant icing to about ½" (1.3cm) thickness.

2 Very lightly rub white fat all over the icing to keep the stamp from sticking; it only takes a thin coating.

3 Firmly press rubber stamps all over the icing, leaving no bare patches.

4 Using your finger and a small amount of gold powder, lightly rub the raised areas of the stamped icing. Repeat as necessary to get a lovely sheen.

To Finish

1 Cut out shapes using the same cookie cutter used for the biscuits.

2 Rub half a lemon over the surface of a cooked biscuit and place an icing rabbit on top. In addition to adding lovely flavor, the lemon juice will help the icing stick to the biscuit.

STRAWBERRY AND ROSE CONSERVE

The fragrant smell of rose gardens and strawberries is well known to participants in the annual Steam Croquet match in Little Puddlington-on-the-Ether. Customarily played as "Gentlemen versus Others," opposing teams have occasionally included automatons, Venusians and even, on one occasion, a monkey butler. The ensuing chaos always draws a large crowd. Rules are often hotly debated, alliances forged and grudges forgiven only for new ones to be made.

The croquet match is an opportunity for gentlemen inventors to see and be seen, for their lady friends to display their biggest hats and finest lace, and for everyone to retire to the pavilion for a fantastic afternoon tea of warm buttered scones with conserve and cream.

Ingredients

575g (1¼ lb.) jam sugar

Juice of ½ lemon

675g (1½ lb.) strawberries cut into ½" (1cm) pieces (if they are only small strawberries, keep them whole)

5ml (1 tsp.) balsamic vinegar

50ml (2 fl. oz.) crème de rose, rose cordial (or a handful of highly scented rose leaves and petals in a muslin bag)

Special Supplies

Four 225ml (8 oz.) jam jars

*Makes four 225ml (8 oz.) jars

TO MAKE THE CONSERVES

1 Place the sugar, lemon juice and strawberries in a large, heavy-bottomed pan. Heat very gently, stirring carefully so as not to crush the strawberries. Continue stirring until the sugar has dissolved.

2 Add the rose leaves and petals if using and boil until the mixture reaches setting point on a jam thermometer, about 20 minutes. (Note the setting point for this conserve will be a thick syrup and not a hard jelly.) Do not stir while the mixture is boiling to keep the strawberries whole.

3 Remove from heat and stir in the balsamic vinegar and crème de rose or cordial (or remove the bag of petals). Leave to stand in the pan for 30 minutes to allow the syrup to thicken and keep the strawberries from floating to the top of the jars.

4 Scrape off any foamy residue on the surface of the jam and spoon into hot jars, sealing immediately with wax disks. Add a lid when cool.

PANTRY PERFECTIONS

Many people question the difference between a conserve, marmalade, jam and jelly. While there are no set definitions, I would suggest the following:

Jelly—A fairly rigidly set delicacy created with just the juice of the fruit.

Jam—A slightly softer set spread made using the whole fruit. It may be sieved to create a smooth, seedless and skinless concoction, or the fruit may be left unsieved complete with pips and texture.

Marmalade—A spread made from citrus fruit that involves using the chopped peel to add interest and flavor.

Conserve—A versatile preserve containing whole or large chunks of fruit in thick syrup, often with other flavors added like liqueurs or spices.

HOUSEKEEPER'S PERKS

For an autumnal picnic on the grounds of your favorite stately home, Bramble gin jelly is the perfect reward for an afternoon's hard blackberry picking. Just follow the instructions below to create 4 jars full for your next soiree!

- Gather 1kg (2¼ lb.) blackberries, 450g (1 lb.) apples, 150ml (¼ pt.) water, 5g (1 tsp.) of juniper berries, 450g (1 lb.) sugar and 100ml (3½ fl. oz.) gin.
- Chop the apples (don't peel or core) and add to a large pan with the blackberries, juniper berries and water. Gently heat and then simmer until all the fruit is thoroughly soft and there is plenty of juice.
- Strain the fruit and juice through a jellybag overnight. Don't squeeze the bag or the juice will go cloudy.
- Measure the juice and return to a clean pan with 450g (1 lb.) of sugar for each 600ml (1 pt.) of juice.
- Stir until the sugar dissolves, then boil fast until it reaches setting point.
- Stir in gin and pour immediately into hot sterilized jars. Cover with a wax disk to cool, then add an airtight lid once the jelly is cold.

TEA TIME TRUFFLES

Just the rustle of a chocolate bar being unwrapped is enough to tear Mr. Woppit away from whatever he happens to be busy with, so this recipe is definitely a favorite. It was first made by an exotic beauty from Bradford who had gained ideas above her station while working as a housemaid for a notable antiquary in Paris. Her subsequent escape from a life of servitude in a hot air balloon, and her rise to fame as the most successful crinoline maker in all of London is, of course, well known; though, her true identity remains a closely guarded secret to this day.

Despite being mobbed by newspaper boys whenever her lofty designs are escorted to a new owner, she still makes time to have tea with her friends once a fortnight, where Mr. Woppit flirts outrageously.

Ingredients

FOR THE TRUFFLES

15g (1 tbsp.) fragrant Rose Pouchong loose black tea

120ml (4 fl. oz.) boiling water

200g (7 oz.) milk chocolate

200g (7 oz.) dark chocolate

300ml (10 fl. oz.) double cream

FOR DECORATION

Iridescent dust, cocoa powder or icing sugar

TO MAKE THE TRUFFLES

1 Place the tea in a cup, then pour the boiling water over it. Leave to steep for 5 minutes while you chop the chocolate into chunks.

2 Place the double cream in a pan and add the brewed tea (without straining) and bring to the boil.

3 Simmer on very low heat for 5 minutes, then strain the cream through a fine sieve into a medium-sized heatproof bowl, discarding the tea leaves.

4 Add the chocolate and stir until completely dissolved, then beat with a wooden spoon until smooth and glossy. Allow to cool completely, then place in the fridge overnight to set.

5 Scoop out teaspoon-sized pieces and, working quickly with hands cooled under cold water, shape into balls. Place the balls onto a baking tin.

6 Drop each truffle into the small bowl of iridescent dust and roll quickly between your palms before placing in a petit four case. Keep the truffles in the refrigerator, removing 30 minutes before serving (15 minutes if it is a hot day).

PANTRY PERFECTIONS

There are many delicious teas available, all of which will impart their own particular flavor to the truffle. For a wonderfully smoky, exotic sweet flavor, try Russian caravan. Or, for more of a citrus note, use a good quality Earl Grey flavored with bergamot oil. Some particular blends such as Twining's Earl Grey with Lavender or the East India Company's Bombay Chai are very delicious with chocolate. Serve these treats alongside cups of tea from the same blend.

HOUSEKEEPER'S PERKS

Try rolling the truffles in cocoa powder for a dark, sophisticated extravagance. You could also try icing sugar, sugar strands or edible glitter.
For an indulgent dark chocolate truffle, replace the 200g (7 oz.) milk chocolate with an extra 200g (7 oz.) dark chocolate. For a lighter, sweeter truffle replace the 200g (7 oz.) dark chocolate with 200g (7 oz.) white chocolate.

Tipsy Turvey Tea Bread

Lady Elsie's recipe is a closely guarded secret, passed down through the family as a legacy from Lady Violet. Its glorious crumbly texture has been known to divert gardeners from re-painting roses and urchins from chimney-cleaning duties, and when the Red Queen came for tea she was thoroughly distracted and quite forgot to demand anybody's head!

Each member of the household has a favorite method for its consumption. It is eaten cold and sliced and spread with butter by the dashing eldest, and warm with ice cream by the naughty youngest. The butler loves the way Cook makes any leftovers into bread and butter pudding, and even the bear in the hall of Sherwood Manor was once found to be clutching a slice slathered in marmalade in his sticky paw!

Ingredients

115g (4 oz.) mixed dried fruit

115g (4 oz.) caster sugar

150ml (¼ pt.) hot tea

3g (⅔ tbsp.) marmalade

1 egg

225g (8 oz.) self-rising flour

TO MAKE THE TEA BREAD

1 Place the dried fruit and sugar in a large bowl, then pour the hot tea over the mixture. Leave overnight, or for at least 6 hours.

2 Preheat the oven to gas mark 4 (350° F/180° C) and line a 450g (1 lb.) loaf tin with grease-proof paper.

3 Add the marmalade, egg and flour to the cooled fruit mixture and combine well. You can use a mixer, but a wooden spoon works just as well.

4 Pour the mixture into the tin. Bake for 50 minutes or until a skewer inserted in the center comes out clean.

5 Remove from tin and cool on a wire rack before slicing.

HOUSEKEEPER'S PERKS

For the perfect cup of tea to go with your perfectly delightful tea bread, why not try making your own flavored sugar lumps? These are a lovely way to add a subtle flavor to a cup of tea or cocktail. All you need to start is a flexible silicone ice cube mold, some caster sugar and a suitable flavor. My favorites include lavender, rose and mint.

To make the lumps, put 55g (2 oz.) of caster sugar and 30g (2 heaping tbsp.) of the flavoring agent (lavender flowers, rose petals, mint leaves, etc.) into a grinder or blender. Add two drops of a food coloring and pulse until the mixture resembles damp sand. Press teaspoons of the mixture into the ice cube mold, firmly packing each one and dusting any excess from around the edges. Leave to dry out completely somewhere warm, like an airing cupboard, for a few days. Unmold carefully and store in an airtight tin until needed.

SCULLERY STORIES

Tea was such an expensive commodity in the early days of its import that even when the brew became cold in the pot, every last bit of it was used up. By soaking dried fruit overnight in the last of the tea, it restored a delicious plumpness and imparted a delicate flavor.

Many different regions of England developed their own tea loaf or tea bread recipes such as the Bara Brith of Wales or Yorkshire Brack. They are not really bread loaves as they generally contain no yeast and taste more like a delicate, fatless fruitcake.

HOUSEKEEPER'S PERKS

If the sun is over the yardarm, and you fancy a tipple with your tea bread, why not try a Paddington Cocktail?

For two servings you will need: 4 measures of gin, 2 measures of marmalade (the runnier the better) and the juice of 1 lime.

Fill a cocktail shaker with ice, add cocktail ingredients and shake well until a frost forms on the outside of the shaker. Strain into glasses half filled with crushed ice. Garnish with a twist of lime peel.

Different types of marmalade will give a different character to this cocktail. For example, The Admiral's Marmalade (p. 104) adds warm treacle Caribbean flavors, while lemon marmalade (p. 89) creates a light citrus drink.

Magical Fruit Scones

As the balloon swept dangerously close to the ground, a cry of "drop the ballast! Quickly!" went up. First went the heavy urn of tea, then the croquet set, followed by the traveling games compendium. Mr. Woppit's friends and relations raced along in the shadow, calling encouragement and pausing to gather the abandoned items. More objects flew from the basket—a jar of jam, then a pair of bloomers caught like a flag from a trailing rope, but Miss Dashwood leapt to defend the hamper. "Not the scones! Never the scones!"

A gust of wind flicked the balloon high into the air as, with a final burst of the burner, it cleared the tree tops and sailed off, scones still onboard, much to the disappointment of the onlookers.

Ingredients

5g (1 tsp.) baking powder

225g (8 oz.) self-rising flour

Pinch of salt

55g (2 oz.) butter

40g (1½ oz.) sugar

115g (4 oz.) mixed dried fruit, the more interesting the better (I used dried raspberries and apricots)

150 ml (5 fl. oz.) coconut milk

*Makes 8 scones

PANTRY PERFECTIONS

Look for really fun dried or semi-dried fruits to use in this recipe. Dried cherries and mango go well together, as do dried blueberries and raspberries. I'd suggest using just two types of fruit so as not to confuse the flavors too much. The coconut milk gives it a richness rather than an overwhelming coconut flavor, so you can always add 15g (1 tbsp.) of desiccated coconut if you want to up the coconut flavor element.

If you want to dry some fruit yourself, choose unblemished fruit. Cut into pieces as necessary and soak in equal amounts of lemon juice and water for 10 minutes. Cover a deep tin tightly with muslin to make a hammock of sorts. Arrange the fruit on the muslin without touching. Place in a very cool oven (140° F/60° C)) for about 5 hours, turning several times during desiccation. Small pieces of fruit like raspberries will dry much faster than a whole peach! Remember, the fruit will shrink hugely when dried—a raisin is just a dried grape, after all!

TO MAKE THE SCONES

1 Heat the oven to gas mark 6 (400° F/ 200° C) and grease a baking tray.

2 In a large bowl, mix together the baking powder, flour and salt. Rub the butter into the flour until it resembles fine sand. Then, stir in the sugar and fruit until thoroughly blended.

3 Make a well in the center of the dry ingredients and pour in the milk. Stir with a spoon until it becomes too sticky, then use a cutting and folding motion with the spoon to blend in the final bits of flour.

4 Pat the dough into a 7" × 7" (18cm × 18cm) grid on a floured board [the dough will be about 1" (2.5cm) deep]. Cut 6 heart-shaped scones.

5 Place scones on the greased tray with plenty of room around each scone. Bake for 12–15 minutes or until golden and crisp on the outside but soft and melting on the inside. Slightly cool on a wire rack. Serve while still warm enough to melt a spread of butter.

J. March

BRIXEN.

CHAPTER FOUR

REGIMENTAL LUNAR ENCAMPMENT ON MARS

Dear Brigadier,

A terrible sight greeted me as my escape pod hatch opened and revealed the arid landscape in front of me. I had been looking forward to a genteel rescue, involving dashing men in uniform, perhaps a regimental dinner or two and then a tour of the excavations before hopping on the next transport home.

Martians to the right of them, Martians to the left of them, our gallant heroes bravely defended the tea table from the clutches of the cake-hungry fiends. One taste of tea and the troops were reinvigorated, prepared to sacrifice not one biscuit to the marauding aliens.

The first lunar regiment on Mars stood firm in their red coats, determined that the fearsome beasts should not interrupt the mining of sugar or stop the flow of tea to the Empire. Bravely, they beat them back, though the beasts' desire for cake was terrible to behold.

So, if you could send some reinforcements— The First Tea Company would be perfect—and maybe another crate of Assam, it would be most appreciated.

With Love,
Emilly

THE FIRST LUNAR REGIMENT requests the pleasure of your company for High Tea in the Officers' Mess.

The regiment is currently enjoying the extensive views across the Tharsis Montes, whose mild volcanic activity can be seen to enliven the skyline. The encampment perimeter is secure, but personal defence devices are suggested just in case of Martian interest.

Please do not forget your breathing apparatus and escape pod in case of emergency evacuation from the area.

RSVP

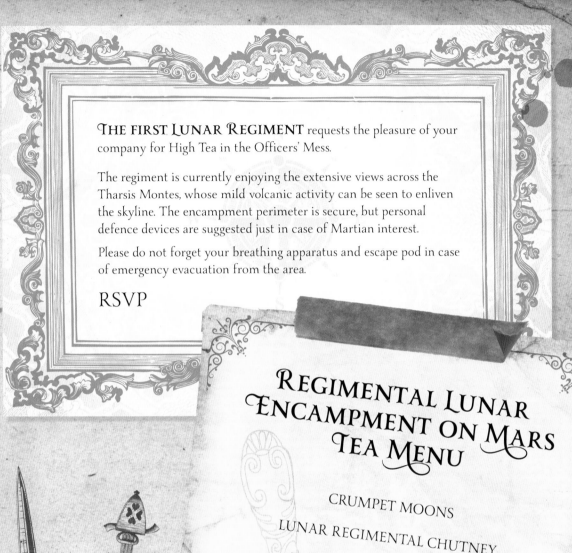

REGIMENTAL LUNAR ENCAMPMENT ON MARS TEA MENU

CRUMPET MOONS

LUNAR REGIMENTAL CHUTNEY

EMPIRE ROCKET CUPCAKES

HARLECH CAKES

PITH HELMET FANCIES

– ALSO CONSIDER SERVING –

CHEESEBOARD WITH CAMEMBERT AND WHITE STILTON WITH GINGER

PLATTER OF EXOTIC FRUIT (STAR FRUIT, DRAGON FRUIT, ETC.)

RUBY PORT

ASSAM TEA

CRUMPET MOONS

Her Majesty's Flying Rocket Squadron is very fond of Crumpets; there is a long history of its admiration being immortalized in art on the sides of airships and dirigibles. Sometimes, these pictures may take the form of an attractive young lady displaying the crumpet on a toasting fork while clad in a Martian regimental bathing suit. Likewise, they occasionally show an attractive young lady about to spread a crumpet with butter and jam before getting dressed in her Martian regimental overalls.

There have also been several tea duels over the identity of the models; although, the First Tea Lord has attempted to keep an eye on both these pictures and the primary sketches, threatening court martial for any he feels lack artistic integrity.

Ingredients

300ml (½ pt.) milk

5g (1 level tsp.) dried yeast

5g (1 tsp.) caster sugar

1.25g (¼ tsp.) salt

5g (1 tsp.) baking powder

225g (8 oz.) plain flour

1 egg, beaten

5g (1 tsp.) bicarbonate of soda (baking soda)

175ml (6 fl. oz.) luke warm water

Special Supplies

Crumpet rings

*Makes 8 crumpets

TO MAKE THE CRUMPETS

1 Heat the milk to body temperature. Add the yeast and sugar and stir. Leave the mixture in a warm place (such as an airing cupboard) for 20 minutes to activate the yeast. It will appear frothy when ready.

2 In a large bowl, mix the salt and baking powder with the flour. Create a well in the center of the flour and stir in the yeasty milk followed by the beaten egg. Cover with a tea towel and leave to proof somewhere warm for 30–45 minutes.

3 In a separate cup, mix the bicarbonate of soda with the water. Gently fold this mixture into the bowl of batter, being careful not to beat it. Leave to rest somewhere warm for 10 minutes.

PANTRY PERFECTIONS

Crumpets are the ideal treat to cook on the boiler of a traveling steam vehicle. It may take a couple of attempts to establish the correct amount of heat and time for cooking, but there's no better way to keep the driver cheery than to hand her a nicely browned and buttery snack. You can place the dough directly on the boiler, or you can place a layer of tinfoil down first if your surface is particularly oily or grimy.

4 Preheat crumpet rings on a griddle over low heat, then spoon the batter into the rings to a depth of about ½" (1.3cm). Make sure you don't fill the rings too full, as the batter will rise as it cooks. Likewise, filling the rings too full will keep the bubbles from forming properly.

Cook for about 5 minutes until the batter is nearly set with plenty of bubbles on the surface. The crumpets should be light brown underneath and have pulled away from the sides of the rings.

5 Remove the crumpets from the rings. Place crumpets back onto the griddle, the other way up, for a minute or two to finish cooking the top. Cool completely on a wire tray.

6 To serve, toast both sides lightly and spread with butter.

PANTRY PERFECTIONS

As well as being eaten with butter and jam, a crumpet also makes the most delicious savoury base for cheese on toast or a mini pizza. Toast the crumpet until warm, then spread the top section with a spoonful of a tomato sauce or chutney of your choice. Grate a liberal layer of your favorite cheese over the top and place under the grill until the cheese is bubbling.

Lunar Regimental Chutney

Transporting stores across the vast ether has always been a bit of a problem. Some things transport extremely well; take cigars and brandy, for example. Tomatoes, on the other hand, do not flourish on Mars, and despite the Horticultural Corps' best attentions, species after species "went native," sneaking off to grow with the red weed and becoming disreputable and inedible.

And so it turned out that the only way of preserving the deliciousness of the tomato was to make them into chutney, which could be distributed amongst the troops for use in sandwiches. Obviously, at the officers' table, it is served daintily in atmospheric sealed chambers with a cheeseboard and port.

Ingredients

20g (4 tsp.) whole seeds of pickling spice mix

1 onion

2 large cooking apples (approximately 450g or 1 lb.)

1 kg (2¼ lbs) tomatoes

350g (12 oz.) tomatillos (just use more tomatoes if you can't find tomatillos)

100g (3½ oz.) dates (stoned)

500g (18 oz.) dark brown sugar

2.5g (½ tsp.) chili flakes

2.5g (½ tsp.) salt

2.5g (½ tsp.) ground ginger

600ml (1 pt.) vinegar

100g (3½ oz.) sultanas (or raisins)

Special Supplies

Muslin and string

5 large jam jars with lids

Wax disks

*Makes 5 jars

To Make the Chutney

1 Tie up the pickling spice mix in a muslin bag, securing tightly with a bit of string.

2 Chop the onion, apples, tomatoes, tomatillos and dates finely into approximately ¼" (6mm) pieces.

3 Place the sugar, muslin bag, chili flakes, salt, ground ginger and vinegar in a very large pan. Cook on low heat and stir with a wooden spoon until the sugar dissolves.

4 Add the chopped vegetables and fruit, along with sultanas, to the pan and stir until it reaches a gentle simmer. Simmer on low heat for approximately 1 hour or until very thick. Stir occasionally at first, then more frequently as it thickens to prevent burning or any sticking on the bottom of the pan.

When you think it is ready, give it a final stir. The chutney should not immediately run back into the path left by the spoon as you move it across the bottom of the pan. The thickness it is now is the thickness it will remain in the jar; it won't "set" any more the way that jam does once placed in the jar.

5 Pour into prepared sterilized jars and seal with wax disks immediately. Add an airtight lid when cool.

SCULLERY STORIES

Chutney is a word that originates in India, along with *pyjama*, *gymkhana*, *thug*, *bangle* and *bazaar*. In 1872, Colonel Yule and AC Burnell created "Hobson Jobson: A glossary of colloquial Anglo-Indian words and phrases." Chutney is included in this useful and entertaining dictionary as "a kind of strong relish made of a number of condiments and fruits, etc." The enormous variety of spiced Indian chutneys brought home to England took Victorian cuisine by storm. Favorite recipes and patented imports abounded, with each Indian province having its own specialty, wet, dry, hot, fragrant, sweet or sour.

HOUSEKEEPER'S PERKS

A jar of brinjal pickle makes a lovely substitute for chutney. To make this delicacy, you will need the following:

10g (2 tsp.) salt
1kg (2¼ lbs.) aubergines chopped into roughly 1" (2.5cm) pieces
700ml (1¼ pt.) oil
5g (1 tsp.) chili powder
10g (2 tsp.) cumin seeds
1.25g (¼ tsp.) mustard seeds
5g (1 tsp.) fenugreek seeds
5g (1 tsp.) turmeric
3 cloves garlic finely chopped
10g (2 tsp.) peeled and finely chopped ginger
½ onion
200g (7 oz.) soft brown sugar
500ml (18 fl. oz.) vinegar

Sprinkle the salt over the aubergine and leave for 30 minutes. While heating oil in a pan, grind all the dry spices together using a pestle and mortar. Once finished, fry the spices along with the garlic and ginger for just 1 minute, stirring all the time.

Add the onion and aubergine and continue cooking for a couple of minutes until the onion is softened. Remove from the heat as you add the sugar and vinegar. Stir well and return to heat on a low simmer until the aubergine is soft and the mixture thick. Pot in sterilized jars.

Empire Rocket Cupcakes

The First Lunar Regiment marches on its stomach! Not literally, of course, that would be silly; but they are second only to The First Tea Company in their devotion to Duty and Cake. A cake that reminds them of the fragrant green world of Earth and its bounteous flower gardens is particularly welcome on this arid, alien world.

Officer Cadet Miss Alice can often be found slowly savoring the violet icing from a cupcake, daydreaming designs for better defences, while Officer Cadet Master Max Esquire checks the camp perimeter for Martian weed encroachments.

Ingredients

FOR THE CUPCAKES

115g (4 oz.) butter

115g (4 oz.) caster sugar

115g (4 oz.) self-rising flour

2 large eggs

30ml (2 tbsp.) milk

5ml (1 tsp.) violette essence [or 5ml (1 tsp.) milk]

FOR THE ICING

50g (1¼ oz.) unsalted butter

80g (2¾ oz.) icing sugar

15ml (1 tbsp.) crème de violette, violet syrup or cordial (or a few drops of flavored essence)

1–3 drops of purple food coloring

FOR THE ICING ROCKETS

White fat or shortening

55g (2 oz.) royal icing mix (this is a special blend of icing sugar that sets very hard)

Approximately 30ml (2 tbsp.) water

Red and yellow food coloring

Iridescent gold powder

5ml (1 tsp.) clear alcohol such as gin or vodka

FOR DECORATION

Edible gold stars, sprinkles, bullets. etc.

Special Supplies

Decorative cupcake cases or paper liners

A4 drawing paper

Deli paper or grease-proof paper

Cling film (plastic wrap)

Piping bag with a large star nozzle and medium writing nozzle

*Makes 12 cupcakes

TO MAKE THE CUPCAKES

1 Preheat the oven to gas mark 5 (375° F/190° C). Place 12 cupcake cases (paper liners) in a muffin or tart tin.

2 In a large bowl, cream the butter and sugar together until pale in color, light and fluffy.

3 Add the flour, eggs, milk and violette flavoring and mix thoroughly, being careful not to overmix.

4 Place about 10ml (2 tsp.) of the mixture into each cupcake case, distributing the batter evenly among all the cases.

5 Bake for 10–15 minutes until the cupcakes have risen and they spring back when pressed in the middle.

For the Icing

1 Beat the butter until light and fluffy.

2 Add the sifted icing sugar and violet flavoring, slowly stirring at first to mix well. Then, add the coloring a drop at a time until you reach the desired shade of purple.

3 Place the icing in a piping bag with a large star nozzle. Swirl rosettes on top of the cakes.

PANTRY PERFECTIONS

Why not experiment with alternate colors and flavorings inspired by different planets? For example, you could make a delightful orange-tasting sponge for Saturn. Just substitute the crème de violette in the recipe for orange juice or cointreau and decorate with orange icing and, perhaps, a royal icing shape of Saturn, complete with rings. How about peppermint for Venus? Substitute peppermint cordial this time and color the icing a pretty green. Instead of an icing rocket, create a silvery moon, or a star or even an air kraken for decoration! A very sophisticated cupcake could be created for Pluto, using Kahlua or liquid coffee essence, with black colored butter icing and a white icing rocket with silver stars!

To Create the Icing Rockets

1 Draw some rockets on a piece of A4 paper. Make heavy marks so you will be able to see through a piece of deli paper or grease-proof paper placed on top. Rub the deli paper or grease-proof paper with a thin layer of white fat (like Trex) so the icing won't stick to the paper when it's time to peel it away.

2 Mix up a fairly stiff blend of royal icing, adding water just a drop at a time to the royal icing mix. Divide it in half and add red coloring to one half and yellow to the other. Place cling film over the containers (letting it touch the icing) so it doesn't dry out.

3 Put a few spoonfuls of the thick red icing in a piping bag with a medium writing nozzle. Pipe the outlines by tracing the images visible beneath the paper. Don't forget details like portholes. Leave to set. Meanwhile, add enough water to the remaining red icing to make a runnier mix.

4 When the outlines are dry, flood the main areas with the runnier icing. I usually use a grease-proof bag with the tip cut off for this (see YouTube video). Leave to dry overnight, then add any tiny rivet details with the thicker icing.

5 Paint the yellow areas with gold powder mixed with a tiny bit of alcohol. Allow to dry, then gently peel away from the backing paper.

Insert rockets into the cupcake icing. Add edible gold stars for extra flare!

Harlech Cakes

The rousing sound of the 45th Cavors male voice choir often lifts spirits among the First Lunar Regiment. Mainly known as a dirigible corp, sometimes during moments of low cloud cover, their singing has been mistaken for that of a heavenly choir. And, on that fateful afternoon when the shout rang out, "Martians, Sir, thousands of them!" the voices of the 45th rose as one, restoring hope to the officers and inspiring many acts of bravery.

This particular delicacy is a favorite amongst the men. Often baked by wives and sweethearts for eating while on maneuvers, its popularity has now spread to other regiments where it is humorously known after The Cavor's favorite song.

Ingredients

FOR THE MARMALADE

*It is not necessary to make your own marmalade. Feel free to use a ready-made jar of your favorite jam or marmalde if you prefer.

2.4L (4 pt.) water

900g (2 lb.) lemons

1.8kg (4 lb.) granulated sugar

FOR THE CAKES

85g (3 oz.) butter or margarine

225g (8 oz.) plain flour

85g (3 oz.) caster sugar

A pinch of salt

85g (3 oz.) sultanas

30g (2 tbsp.) lemon marmalade

1 egg

15ml (1 tbsp.) milk

Special Supplies

Muslin and string

6 medium jam jars with lids

3" (7.5cm) cutter

1" (2.5cm) cutter (for center holes)

*Makes 6 jars

To Make Lady B's Marmalade

Note: If using a jar of ready-made marmalade, please skip ahead to the instructions on page 91.

1 Measure the water into a pan. Cut the lemons in half and squeeze out the juice in a bowl.

2 In another bowl, scrape out any pips and pith and put them into a muslin bag secured with string. Add the juice to the water.

3 Cut the peel into strips. I prefer thin strips, but you can use chunky strips if you like. Strip any pith you can off the peel and add it to the muslin bag. Don't worry if some pith gets left behind; it will dissolve in the boiling process.

4 Add the peel and the muslin bag to the water and juice mixture, tying the muslin bag to the handle of the pan so it stays in place. Bring up to boiling and simmer gently for about an hour until the peel is soft. Remove the muslin bag of pips and place it to the side in a bowl.

5 Add the sugar and stir until all the crystals have disappeared. Increase the heat to high. Squeeze the cooled muslin bag over the pan. It should ooze its pectin out; if not, don't worry, as it's probably in the mix already.

6 Stir everything together. Bring the mixture to a boil and allow the liquid to rapidly boil for approximately 15 minutes (occasional stirring is acceptable). Test for set using the instructions in the tip bar below. If your mixture has not reached the setting point, boil for another 5–10 minutes and test again.

7 Once it's reached the setting point, take the marmalade off the heat. Allow to settle for 20 minutes before putting into sterilized, warmed jars and sealing. Wait at least one full day before using the marmalade to make the harlech cakes.

PANTRY PERFECTIONS

To test for set of jams and marmalades, use this handy trick:
· Pop several saucers into the freezer ahead of time to chill the plates.
· Once your preserve has boiled for roughly the correct amount of time, remove one of the saucers from the freezer. Drop a small amount of the mixture onto the cold plate. (Meanwhile, be sure to remove the pan from the heat so you don't overboil it.)
· Allow the mixture to rest on the chilled saucer for about a minute, then push it around the plate with your finger. The mixture should begin to flake or gel as it moves.
· If it doesn't, continue to boil the preserves, testing every 5–10 minutes on a fresh chilled saucer.

To Make the Cakes

1 Rub the butter into the flour until the mixture resembles fine bread crumbs. Add in sugar, salt, sultanas and marmalade and stir thoroughly.

2 Add the egg and the milk to the mixture, making a very stiff dough.

3 Pat out or roll the dough on a lightly floured board to about ½" (1.3cm) thickness. Cut out rounds with a 3" (7.5cm) cutter. To make rings, use a 1" (2.5cm) cutter to remove the centers.

After removing rings, either re-roll offcuts to make more cakes, or bake the little circles to serve as tiny petit fours.

4 Cook the rings on a griddle over low heat for 1–2 minutes or until golden brown on one side. Flip over with a palette knife. They aren't ruined if they catch a little, but do keep an eye on them. They should be a little soft in the center, but not completely raw. Adjust your griddle temperature as necessary.

5 While these are delicious cold, they are definitely best eaten after cooling on a wire rack for only a couple of minutes, while still warm and gooey in the middle.

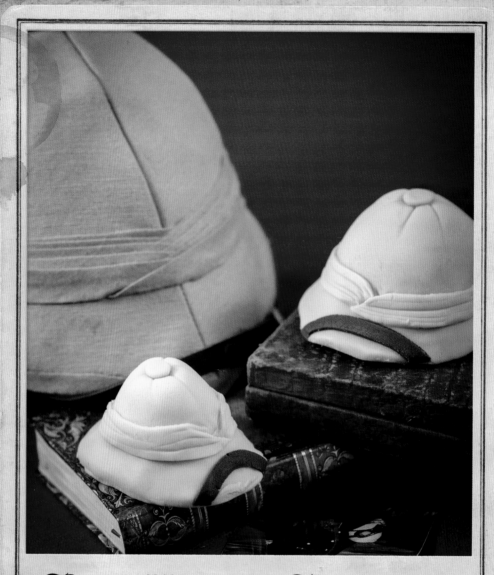

PITH HELMET FANCIES

Upon the rocky outpost overlooking the plains, one figure is silhouetted against the sky; cup in hand, the hero of the battle of Amazonis Platinia keeps watch. In the arid heat of Mars, the soldier's brass-lined pith helmet is the only thing that can stand between him and the controlling thought waves of the original inhabitants. It was Lieutenant Colonel Lawless Latham who first discovered the creatures' antipathy of lemons.

Supplies were instantly shipped in from the Amalfi Groves, and disrupter rays were re-fitted to mist a fine spray of lemon juice, which kept the blighters at bay. However, the entire camp was soaked and the taste of lemon pervaded everything, even the Colonel's favorite ginger cakes!

Ingredients

FOR THE CUPCAKES

100ml (3½ fl. oz.) boiling water

15g (1 tbsp.) loose leaf Earl Grey tea

85g (3 oz.) butter

115g (4 oz.) sugar

115g (4 oz.) self-rising flour

2 eggs

Heaped dessert spoon of finely chopped crystallized ginger

FOR THE ICING

50g (1¾ oz.) unsalted butter

80g (2¾ oz.) icing sugar

5g (1 tsp.) finely grated lemon zest

5ml (1 tsp.) lemon juice [or 2.5ml (½ tsp.) lemon essence]

TO FINISH

Small pack of white or cream ready-to-roll icing or rolled fondant

Sugar flower petal paste

*Makes 12 cupcakes

TO MAKE THE CUPCAKES

1 Preheat the oven to gas mark 5 375° F/190° C). Place 12 cupcake cases in a muffin or tart tin.

2 Pour the boiling water over the tea in a mug or cup and let steep for 5 minutes.

3 In a large bowl, cream the butter and the sugar together until pale in color, light and fluffy. I use a wooden spoon, but an electric mixer is fine, too.

4 Add the flour, the egg and the strained tea, mixing slowly but thoroughly. Stir in the chopped crystallized ginger until it is evenly distributed throughout the mixture.

5 Place about 10ml (2 tsp.) of mixture into each cupcake case. Bake for 10-15 minutes until the cupcakes have risen and spring back when pressed in the middle.

FOR THE ICING

1 Beat the butter until light and fluffy with a wooden spoon or an electric mixer.

2 Add the sifted icing sugar, lemon zest and juice. Mix by hand at first to prevent icing sugar from spraying everywhere!

PANTRY PERFECTIONS

Lemon and ginger is a classic combination, but oranges or limes also work in this recipe. Simply substitute the lemon zest and juice in the butter icing for either orange or lime zest and juice.

To Add the Fondant

1 Remove the paper cases and slice the tops off the cupcakes so they lay flat.

2 Turn the cupcakes upside down and slice a little off each side to create oval shapes.

3 Add a spoonful of butter icing to each top, smoothing it into the classic pith helmet domed shape. Scrape a little icing over the cake, too, as this will seal in the moistness and provide a good grip for the fondant. When you have a good shape, put them somewhere cool to set firm for a couple of hours.

4 Color the ready-to-roll icing with a little yellow and black to get a good sandy color for the pith helmets. Add tiny bits of color to the fondant using a cocktail stick. Knead in thoroughly before adding additional color.

5 Roll out the icing to about ¹/₁₆" (2mm) thickness and cut circles large enough to cover the cakes. Be sure to leave a little extra for the hat brim.

HOUSEKEEPER'S PERKS

For a quicker teatime treat, you can also make simple cupcakes. Make the cake mix and bake as directed. Leave the cakes in their cases and decorate with a swirl of the lemon butter icing and a scattering of crystallized ginger. Fine grating of lemon zest or a little white chocolate molded cog would also look lovely.

6 Gently lift and place the icing on the cupcake, smoothing over with your hand until it forms a good cover. Trim round the edges, leaving a brim of about ½" (1.3cm).

7 Add details modeled from a mixture of equal amounts of ready-to-roll icing and sugar flower paste blended together.

PANTRY PERFECTIONS

Modeling tools can be created from all sorts of handy kitchen implements. I use a cocktail stick to impress lines in icing and also to texture with small dots. A flat, unserrated blade is best for cutting strips of icing, while button shapes can be formed by breaking off tiny pieces of icing and rolling them gently between the fingers. If you find the icing is sticking as you roll it out, try rubbing a tiny bit of white vegetable fat or shortening on your work surface, fingers or tools. Use a tiny paintbrush dipped in water to glue icing decorations to the main covering.

SCHRIVER & KIBLER

1213 N. 3RD ST.,
HARRISBURG, PA

CHAPTER FIVE
VOYAGE FROM THE DEEPS

Dear Mr. Rivet,

Your old shipmate, Admiral Saunders, sends his regards and he hopes you managed to get the squid ink out of your shirt in the end. We have been traveling at quite some speed and, indeed, depth, marveling at all manner of aquatic life. This has been a most successful research trip in finding a suitable spot to build the new Mariana hub; it's all terribly exciting.

The Submersible has a wide assortment of surveying equipment on board as well as an alarming amount of weaponry. I am informed they are for engaging pirate vessels only, and most creatures we have met so far seem more inquisitive than hostile, though there's always a first time. . . .

The crew has been jolly friendly, and we often get together in the afternoons for a spot of tea and a sporting game or two. The ship's engineers aboard the *Naughty Lass* are a particularly feisty bunch; I know you would approve of both their ingenuity and their devotion to cheese scones.

Much love,
Emilly

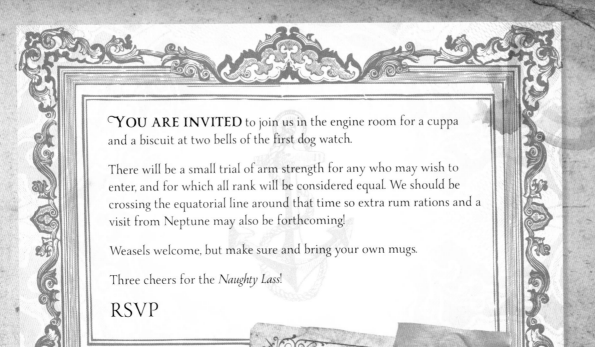

YOU ARE INVITED to join us in the engine room for a cuppa and a biscuit at two bells of the first dog watch.

There will be a small trial of arm strength for any who may wish to enter, and for which all rank will be considered equal. We should be crossing the equatorial line around that time so extra rum rations and a visit from Neptune may also be forthcoming!

Weasels welcome, but make sure and bring your own mugs.

Three cheers for the *Naughty Lass*!

RSVP

VOYAGE FROM THE DEEPS MENU

MR. RIVET'S CHEESE AND CHILI SCONES

ADMIRAL'S MARMALADE

NAUTILUS SHIP BISCUITS

ABSINTHE COG BISCUITS

MR. BRUNEL'S FAVORITE FUDGE

– ALSO CONSIDER SERVING –

HOT BUTTERED TOAST

FRESH FRUIT

CHEESEBOARD WITH BRIE AND LANCASHIRE

GUNPOWDER OR ENGLISH BREAKFAST TEA

Mr. Rivet's Cheese and Chili Scones

A mysterious lady once told Mr. Rivet that he would find happiness through the color yellow. Taking her advice to heart, he attempted to find joy in all manner of outlandish devices–canary-colored racing cars, lemon cravats, and he even insisted on painting the door to Dickens and Rivet a bright mustard hue. However, it was not until one day, voyaging as a guest aboard the *Naughty Lass*, that a plate of golden scones caught his eye, and a look of bliss spread across his face.

Mr Woppit likes them cold as picnic scones, and claims they are especially delicious if made into sandwiches with a filling of fresh rocket or watercress. He does tend to only eat the watercress or rocket, but Mr. Rivet is always happy to finish off the rest.

Ingredients

55g (2 oz.) butter or margarine

225g (8 oz.) self-rising flour

5g (1 tsp.) baking powder

Pinch of salt

5g (1 tsp.) dried flaked mild chili

5g (1 tsp.) smoked paprika

2.5g (½ tsp.) chili powder (add more or less powder to taste)

1.25g (¼ tsp.) rough ground black pepper

140g (5 oz.) coarse grated mature Cheddar cheese

150ml (5 fl. oz.) milk

*Makes 8 scones

TO MAKE THE SCONES

1 Preheat the oven to gas mark 6 (400° F/200° C) and lightly grease a baking tray.

2 In a large bowl, rub the butter or margarine into the flour until it resembles fine sand.

3 Stir in all of the dry ingredients, including the cheese, until thoroughly blended. Make a well in the center of the mixture and pour in the milk. Stir with a spoon until it becomes too sticky, then use a cutting and folding motion with the spoon to blend in the final bits of flour.

4 Pat the dough into a 7" × 7" (18cm × 18cm) grid on a floured board [the dough will be about 1" (2.5cm) deep]. Use a sharp knife to cut a 3" × 3" (7.5cm × 7.5cm) grid, yielding 9 scones.

5 Place the scones on the greased tray, leaving plenty of room around each scone. Bake for 12–15 minutes until golden and crisp on the outside and soft and melting on the inside.

6 Remove the scones from the tray and cool on a wire rack.

PANTRY PERFECTIONS

Scones are always best while still warm. I would suggest eating these about 5–10 minutes after they have come from the oven and are still warm enough to melt the butter. If you cannot eat them directly after baking, I would suggest freezing them once cooled. Then, when you are ready to serve the scones, simply thaw for a couple of hours and reheat in the oven for 5 minutes to re-crisp.

HOUSEKEEPER'S PERKS

If you are not disposed to look favorably on the flavor of chili, an alternative combination is blue cheese and walnut. To make these scones, simply leave out the chili and paprika and replace the Cheddar cheese with 140g (5 oz.) of blue cheese (Stilton or Danish blue). Then, add 115g (4 oz.) of chopped walnuts into the mix.

Fragrant red onion scones are an interesting vegan option, if created with vegan margarine and soya milk. Just add 5g (1 tsp.) cumin seeds, 10g (2 tsp.) garam masala and 115g (4 oz.) of very finely chopped red onion instead of the Ctheddar, chili and paprika.

PANTRY PERFECTIONS

To create a tasty spread, try combining your butter with other condiments and seasonings. The resulting mixture will give an extra level of flavor to your sandwiches and scones. These are the admiral's favorite combinations!

· 15g (1 tbsp.) of salted butter mixed with Bulldog Mustard (pictured here) for an added kick
· 15g (1 tbsp.) of salted butter with 15g (1 tbsp.) of chutney for an aromatic edge
· 15g (1 tbsp.) butter with 1 dessert spoon full of caramelised red onion for a sweet flavor
· 15g (1 tbsp.) butter with 1 dessert spoon full of pesto for an Italian feel
· 15g (1 tbsp.) butter with 5g (1 tsp.) of marmite just for Rolando

ADMIRAL'S MARMALADE

The glorious orangery Mr. Paxton made for the Admiral's House is a thing of beauty. Polished pipes of gleaming brass filled with steam ensure an even temperature is maintained even in the harshest winter. Huge panes of glass capture every moment of sun, in stark contrast to the gloomy depths of the ocean floor.

The oranges grow plump and round until they are plucked by Mrs. Saunders and whipped into heavenly marmalade. The Admiral always likes to have some aboard to spread on his morning toast and dream of home. And as Daisy Saunders always says, an extra tot of rum never does a body any harm.

Ingredients

680g (1½ lb.) oranges (about 3 large oranges)

Juice of 1 lemon

850ml (1½ pt.) water

680g (1½ lb.) light brown demerara sugar

230g (½ lb.) dark brown muscavado sugar

125ml (4 fl. oz.) dark rum

15ml (1 tbsp.) black treacle (blackstrap molasses)

5g (½ oz.) sachet of pectin

Special Supplies

5 small jam jars or 2 large ones with lids

Wax disks

PANTRY PERFECTIONS

Because the alcohol in this marmalade makes setting difficult, I add commercial pectin, which comes in bottles. If you can't find any pectin, you can make your own by boiling crabapples in water and siphoning off the juice. Just use the juice in the recipe instead of water. If you choose to leave out the rum, you shouldn't need extra pectin.

To Make the Marmalade

1 Squeeze the juice from the oranges and place in a very large jam pan along with the lemon juice and the water.

2 Remove the flesh and as much pith as you can from the oranges and place in a muslin bag with the pips from the orange and lemon. Hang the bag in the pan, tying it to a wooden spoon suspended across the pan. The pectin is actually in these parts, so boiling them in the juice assists with the set.

3 Chop the peel into pieces around 1" (2.5cm) long and ⅛" (3mm) wide. Feel free to chop finer or chunkier pieces according to your taste.

4 Boil the peel in the juice and water mixture for about an hour or until very tender. Allow to cool, then remove the muslin bag, squeezing every last drop of pectin goodness from it first.

5 Add both sugars as well as the molasses, pectin and rum, and stir over low heat until dissolved.

6 Bring mixture to a boil. Boil hard at gas mark 7 (425° F/220° C), stirring until a set is reached. If you are using commercial pectin, this will only take about 4 minutes. If you aren't using the pectin, test for set on a cold saucer (see page 90). Leave the marmalade to cool for 10 minutes, then stir to distribute the peel evenly.

7 Place 15ml (1 tbsp.) of rum in the bottom of each sterilized jar and pour in the hot jam.

8 Cover each jar with a wax disk until cool. Replace the disks with lids when cool enough to touch.

105

PANTRY PERFECTIONS

To create a truly unique piece of marmalade history, your jar will need a suitable label. You can use a computer program of your choice to create a delightful design, then simply print onto sticky labels. You could also handwrite your labels and use rubber stamps with a suitable Steampunk design to create a wonderful border.

For an extra touch, prestain your labels with tea. Simply pop a tea bag in a cup and cover with a little boiling water. Allow to cool until the bag can be handled, then squeeze most of the tea from the bag. Using the bag like a sponge, color the paper. Repeat color layers around the edges to give the impression of age. Do not get the paper too wet! Allow the labels to dry thoroughly before printing or writing.

Nautilus Ship Biscuits

As the crew sat at their supper of biscuits and cheese, the two ship's ferrets crept toward the rapidly disappearing crumbs. "You see those weasels, Saunders?" said Mr. O'Brien solemnly. "I do," Saunders replied. "Which would you choose?" O'Brien returned. "There is not a thing to choose between them. They are the same species of Mustelidae, and one does not strike me in any way as superior to the other," answered Mr. Saunders. "But suppose you absolutely had to choose?" his friend persisted. "Then I should choose the right-hand weasel; it has a perceptible advantage in both length and breadth," said Saunders. "There I have you!" cried O'Brien. "You are completely dished, indeed, you are all at sea. Don't you know that in the Submersible Corps you must always choose the lesser of two weasels? Oh ha, ha, ha, ha!"

Ingredients

55g (2 oz.) plain flour

115g (4 oz.) finely ground rolled oats

55g (2 oz.) rolled oats

55g (2 oz.) solid white vegetable fat

5g (1 tbsp.) fresh, finely chopped lemon thyme

5g (1 tbsp.) freshly chopped rosemary

2.5g (½ tsp.) sea salt

2.5g (½ tsp.) rough ground pepper

Approximately 90ml (3 fl. oz.) hot water

Special Supplies

2" (5cm) round cookie cutter

*Makes 24 biscuits

TO MAKE THE BISCUITS

1 Preheat the oven to gas mark 5 (375° F/190° C). Mix the flour and oats together, then rub the fat into the mixture.

2 Stir in the herbs, salt and pepper. Add the hot water and stir until it makes a stiff paste. Add a little more water teaspoon by teaspoon if necessary.

3 On a floured board, roll out the mixture to ¹⁄₁₆" (2mm) thickness, then cut into rounds using a 2" (5cm) cookie cutter. The dough should yield approximately 24 biscuits.

4 Place the biscuits on a tray and bake for 20 minutes or until just golden around the edges.

5 Cool on a wire rack. Once completely cooled, they may be stored in an airtight tin for up to a week.

PANTRY PERFECTIONS

Fresh herbs will add a particularly lovely flavor to this biscuit; however, if you only have access to dried herbs, I suggest using half the quantity, as they are more intense in flavor. Other delicious herb and seed combinations include the following:

· 15g (1 tbsp.) fresh chopped chives and 5g (1 heaped tsp.) black onion (nigella) seeds

· 15g (1 tbsp.) fresh chopped sage and 15g (1 tbsp.) fresh chopped parsley

· 5g (1 tsp.) crushed black pepper and 5g (1 heaped tsp.) fennel seed

· 15g (1 tbsp.) poppy seeds and 15g (1 tbsp.) sesame seeds

· 15g (1 tbsp.) fresh chopped coriander and 5g (1 tsp.) dried chilli flakes

· 15g (1 tbsp.) fresh chopped oregano and 15g (1 tbsp.) fresh chopped basil

· 15g (1 tbsp.) fresh chopped lovage and 15g (1 tbsp.) fresh chopped thyme vulgaris

HOUSEKEEPER'S PERKS

Port and Stilton potted cheese makes a particularly delicious spread for the Nautilus Ship Biscuits. To make this you will need the following:

225g (8 oz.) Stilton, finely grated (if it is a bit old and hard, so much the better!)
55g (2 oz.) butter, softened
30ml (2 tbsp.) ruby port
Salt and pepper to taste

Pound ingredients together using a pestle and mortar, starting with the cheese, adding the butter spoon by spoon, and finally stirring in the port and seasoning to taste. Likewise, you could simply pop the ingredients into an electric blender and pulse until smooth. Press the mixture down into a jar, cover with clarified butter (melted butter that has had the solids float to the top and removed with a teaspoon) and keep in the refrigerator for up to a week.

Absinthe Cog Biscuits

Engineers and gearwheels go together like tea and biscuits. Whenever there is a pause in the engine room of the *Naughty Lass*, the crew may be found designing bigger, better and more complex steam-driven machines, often with the use of these biscuits as visual aids.

Sometimes they prove just too tempting, and a secret nibble of a sprocket completely changes a design. The late night peckishness of Able Seaman George, which destroyed the carefully laid out plans for the Universal Continuum Reverse Leveraging Piston, must serve as a warning to all midnight oil burners.

Ingredients

FOR THE BISCUITS

225g (8 oz.) flour

55g (2 oz.) white vegetable shortening (such as Trex or Cooken)

55g (2 oz.) butter or vegan margarine

115g (4 oz.) sugar

1 dessert spoon of finely ground star anise

FOR THE ICING

100g (3½oz.) icing sugar

Approximately 1 dessert spoon full of absinthe

Several drops of green food coloring

Special Supplies

12" (30.5cm) round cutter, tin or bendable wire (for cog cutters)

Ruler

Masking tape

Straight-edged pliers

Piping bag with medium writing nozzle

*Makes 18 biscuits

TO MAKE THE BISCUITS

1 Preheat the oven to gas mark 6 (400° F/200° C) and lightly grease a baking tray. In a large bowl, cream the vegetable shortening, butter and sugar together with a wooden spoon until pale and fluffy.

2 Slowly add the flour and ground star anise to the creamed mixture, stirring until a firm dough forms. If necessary, add a little water one teaspoon at a time.

3 Transfer the dough ball to the refrigerator and allow it to rest for about an hour or until firm.

4 Roll out on a lightly floured board and cut out shapes with a cog-shaped cutter (see tip bar on page 112). Re-roll any scraps to cut more biscuits, but avoid overworking the dough or it will become tough.

5 Place the biscuits on a baking tray, prick all over with a fork and bake for 8–10 minutes.

6 Cool for 30 seconds on the tray, then transfer to a wire rack to cool completely.

SCULLERY STORIES

There are several methods of drinking absinthe. The French method is the purist's version, dripping ice cold water through a sugar cube balanced on a slotted spoon, allowing the louching process to release additional aromas and flavors. Special absinthe iced water fountains, which slowly drip through elegant brass spigots can even be found.

A more showy method is the Bohemian. The sugar lump is soaked in absinthe and set on the spoon above the glass containing more absinthe. The sugar is set alight, and tipped into the glass, igniting the alcohol, which is doused immediately by a measure of iced water. This is a modern method which burns off most of the alcohol, changing the taste considerably. As such, it is shunned by most serious absinthe devotees.

PANTRY PERFECTIONS

To create a cog-shaped cutter, you first need a very large round cutter, about 12" (30.5cm) in circumference. A flexible tin or a strip of bendable copper would also work. (If using a strip of copper, you will join it together after making the teeth.)

· Place a piece of masking tape around the outside of the cutter and carefully measure it exactly. For a 5-spoke cutter, divide this measurement by 20. For a 6-spoke cutter, divide this measurement by 24. Draw straight lines up the masking tape at these distances. (For a copper strip, be sure to leave an extra mark as an overlap to join it together after making.)

· Take a pair of fairly thin straight-edged pliers and bend the metal at 90° along each mark. You will bend right, right and left, left, repeating the pattern all the way around to create the crenellations.

· To make the center holes in the cookies, simply find a nice, small round cutter to stamp out dough after all the cogs are cut.

FOR THE ICING

1 Mix the icing sugar with enough absinthe and food coloring to make a fine, fairly runny consistency.

2 Place icing in a piping bag with a medium writing nozzle. Drizzle lines across the biscuits in zigzags or stripes. Don't cover too much of the biscuit's surface or the flavor will be overpowering!

3 Leave to set for an hour before consuming. The biscuits will keep well in single layers in a tin for up to a week (if they last that long!).

Mr. Brunel's Favorite Fudge

Mr. Brunel's visit to inspect the newly renovated *Naughty Lass* prior to its first Atlantean reconnaissance was a highlight of the social maritime calendar. The crew lined up in their least scruffy overalls, ready to doff caps and look embarrassed, and the ship's ferrets were washed and brushed.

But it was the sight of a bag of sweetmeats and the chief engineer's fine French pocket watch ticking upon the table that seemed to impress the great man most, even more than the sight of eight specially trained and armored Atlantic squid swimming by with lanterns in their beaks and gilded seaweed in their wake!

Ingredients

55g (2 oz.) butter

450g (1 lb.) sugar

1 tin condensed milk [400ml (14 fl. oz.)]

100 ml (3½ fl. oz.) water

30ml (2 tbsp.) honey

85g (3 oz.) macadamia nuts

TO MAKE THE FUDGE

1 Grease and line a 7" (18cm) tin.

2 Place all ingredients except the nuts in a large pan and stir over gentle heat until the sugar is completely dissolved.

3 Bring to a boil and cook for 7–10 minutes until the mixture is a lovely golden brown. Stir frequently to prevent the sugar from burning.

4 Remove from the heat and beat for 2 minutes until the mixture turns thick and fudgy. Stir in the nuts, then pour the mixture into the tin.

5 While still warm, mark into 1" (2.5cm) squares. When fully cool, cut the rest of the way through the squares.

PANTRY PERFECTIONS

Beating the fudge is quite hard work, so if you have a sprained wrist—or if you're just feeling a little lazy—find two heatproof bowls that fit inside each other with about a 2" (5cm) gap at the base. Fill the bottom bowl with a little boiling water and place the second on top. Pour the mixture into the top bowl and whisk with an electric whisk until it turns into fudge. Pour into tins as instructed in the recipe.

W. Rützler
FOTOGRAF

DORNBIRN
GRABENWEG N° 3.

116

CHAPTER SIX
BLOSSOMS IN SHANGRI-LA

Dear Miss P,

Well, we reached the summit at last! Lady Hardy had all the professor's gadgets ready, and we soon set up Kintup's equipment. The snow was thick on the ground, and there was a bit of a hairy moment with a rambunctious Yeti, but Mr. Woppit and Isaac kept it distracted while we made a rainbow from a profusion of bubbles.

Looking through the colors, we could see that, indeed, there did appear to be a city in the valley which had, until that point, been hidden from our eyes. Passing through one by one, we had soon attracted a crowd of enthusiastic and welcoming residents, who straightaway started to prepare a feast in our honor.

Despite the icy crags that surround it, the Valley is almost tropical, with hot springs that flow past banks full of flowers and new creatures. I have a whole host of things drawn in my sketchbook to share with you! I shall be returning with Dr. Livingstone, who claims he's not been lost at all, merely resting.

Lots of love,
Emilly

YOU ARE BID MOST WELCOME to the Adventurers Club, Shangri-La.

We would be most honored if you would partake of tea with us this afternoon at the clubhouse to celebrate Lady Hardy's ascent of Mount Kailash. We look forward to welcoming all the new visitors and hearing their stories and news.

The clubhouse can be found above the second waterfall, being the third building on the right, with an ornate golden roof.

Come when you can and stay as long as you desire.

RSVP

BLOSSOMS IN SHANGRI-LA TEA MENU

ADVENTURER'S BREAKFAST MUFFINS

TEA EGGS

ORIENTAL GOOSEBERRY AND BLACKCURRANT FRUIT CHEESE

TIME TRAVELER'S TART

PASHA'S CHAI

SHERPA'S CHESTNUTS

PEAR, PARSNIP AND ROSE LOAF CAKE

– ALSO CONSIDER SERVING –

CREAM CHEESE AND CRYSTALLIZED GINGER SANDWICHES

CUCUMBER AND BRINJAL PICKLE SANDWICHES

CHEESEBOARD WITH MANCHEGO, MONTEREY JACK AND FETA

RUSSIAN CARAVAN TEA

ADVENTURER'S BREAKFAST MUFFINS

The lovely princess Victoria, upon hearing there was a new palace chef whose speciality was fresh baked muffins so light they could float away, famously commented, "They had better be good."

Judging by the waistlines of many court members in later years, they jolly well were! The chef, however, having handed on his secret recipes to another generation of kitchen skivvies, craved adventure and, one night, hid aboard an airship bound for India.

The ship never arrived at its destination, but a few months later, adventurers emerging from the Himalayas told tall and improbable tales of a kingdom of milk and muffins, nestled between the inhospitable peaks. In the kitchen of the Adventurers Club, the former royal cook spins yarns of life at court that are every bit as exciting as the adventurer's shaggy Yeti stories.

Ingredients

450g (1 lb.) white bread flour

Pinch of salt

10g (2 tsp.) dried yeast or 30g (6 tsp.) fresh yeast, nicely crumbled

5g (1 tsp.) caster sugar

225ml (8 fl. oz.) warm milk (hand temperature) in a jug

Special Supplies

3" (7.5cm) round cutter

Oil for greasing

Parchment or grease-proof paper

*Makes 8 muffins

To Make the Muffins

1 Grease 12 circles of baking paper slightly larger than your cutter. Place them oiled side up on a baking tray (or two if necessary).

2 Mix the bread flour and salt together in a large bowl.

3 Place the yeast and sugar in the warm milk and stir until dissolved. Leave for 15 minutes in a warm place, until a froth has formed on the top.

4 Make a well in the center of the flour and pour in the liquid. Mix well with a fork first, then lightly by hand. It will be very sticky, but don't worry; just keep scraping it off your fingers and kneading until everything is well mixed and smooth. Leave to rise in a warm place for 30 minutes.

PANTRY PERFECTIONS

There is an etiquette to observe when serving the Adventurer's Breakfast Muffins. Ideally, they should be served warm off the griddle, but they can also be kept warm by judicious use of a muffin warmer. This is a covered dish with an extra hollow under the plate that can be filled with hot water, keeping your muffins fresh all through breakfast.

Likewise, muffins should never be sliced open with a knife; this would destroy the delicate nature of the dough. They should instead be gently split by means of inserting two forks to tear open a slit. Insert butter inside of the slit, then close it up and cut the muffin neatly into two semicircular halves, allowing the butter to ooze out.

If you really cannot eat them immediately, it is permissible to leave them until cold (unsplit). Then, at a more convenient moment, slice the muffin in two with a knife and toast just the cut halves under a grill or in front of a fire. Serve with butter and jam, or a poached egg and hollandaise sauce.

5 Dust your hands with flour and knead dough on a lightly floured board for 5 minutes. Be sure to keep your hands moving so they don't stick to the dough.

6 Roll the dough out on a floured board to ½" (1.3cm) thickness. Cut out rounds and place each round on a baking parchment circle. Leave to rise again for at least an hour but no more than 3 hours.

7 Heat a heavy-bottomed skillet or griddle over the lowest heat possible and brush lightly with oil. Place the muffins very gently on the skillet, lifting each one under the baking parchment with a spatula and flipping at the last minute so the dough side is against the heated metal. After a minute, peel the paper backing off the top.

8 Turn the muffins just once, when the underside is brown, after about 1 minute. All muffins should be fully cooked in the center. Place on the outer part of the griddle to continue if they are still raw.

TEA EGGS

This is an unusual and delicious savory addition to afternoon tea. The spices impart a delicate flavor and beautiful pattern similar to that of marble. The spice mixture may also be saved after the steeping, frozen and used again once or twice.

Hard boil 6 eggs for 10 minutes. Immdiately rinse in cold water until cool enough to touch, then tap them very gently against a hard surface until they are cracked all over, but the membrain is intact.

Boil 600ml (1 pt.) of water with the following ingredients:

    30ml (2 tbsp.) black tea
    3 star anise
    100ml (3¹/₂ fl. oz.) soy sauce
    5g (1 tsp.) fennel seeds
    5g (1 tsp.) cloves
    1 stick cinnamon
    5g (1 tsp.) pepper
    5g (1 tsp.) salt

Steep the cracked eggs in the mixture for 3–6 hours, then peel and serve.

HOUSEKEEPER'S PERKS

To make a cog shaped butter slice, you will need a 2" (5cm) round cutter and a ¹/₂" (1.3cm) round cutter. Cut a slice of butter about ¹/₄" (6mm) thick and place in the freezer between two pieces of deli or greaseproof paper for about an hour.
Remove from the freezer and take away the top piece of paper only. Cut several 2" (5cm) rounds, then cut a small middle hole in each round with the ¹/₂" (6mm) cutter.
Finally use the ¹/₂" (1.3cm) cutter to take out notches all the way around the edge, start at the top, then do a notch opposite.
Take out equal numbers of notches at equal spaces each side to make a gearwheel shape. You can use different sized and shaped cutters for different designs.

Oriental Gooseberry and Blackcurrant Fruit Cheese

Amid the snow and ice of the mountains surrounding the hidden valley, who would have guessed that all manner of exquisite and exotic fruits were but a few yards away? Ripening in the rich sunlight and warmed by the hot springs, nothing can compare to their size and flavor.

This solid, sweet and sharp heart is perfect for slicing thinly and serving with cheese and biscuits whenever expeditions need a pause to admire the view. Lord Kershaw's famous forty peaks attempt was notorious for stopping every mile or so just so the party could enjoy its rations. They returned after conquering only one mountain, as they had run out of Roquefort.

Ingredients

FOR THE FRUIT CHEESE

450g (1 lb.) blackcurrants

450g (1 lb.) gooseberries

150ml (¼ pt.) water

Around 750g (1½ lb.) sugar

FOR DECORATION

Edible gold powder

Special Supplies

Heart-shaped ramekin dishes or molds

Cog-shaped stencils

Brush for applying gold powder

PANTRY PERFECTIONS

If you don't have gooseberries or blackcurrants, you can use all sorts of different fruits to make equally delicious fruit cheeses; however, you do need to make sure that your fruit always has sufficient pectin in it to set.

Fruits high in pectin include cooking and crabapples, red and blackcurrants, quince, cranberries, gooseberries and damsons.

Fruits with a moderate amount of pectin include raspberries, apricots, greengages and early blackberries.

Cherries, pears, rhubarb, strawberries, peaches, blueberries, late blackberries and elderberries are all low in pectin.

For the best combinations, use half high pectin fruit and half low or moderate pectin fruit. Good examples include strawberry and redcurrant, crabapple and rhubarb, and even quince and apricot.

TO MAKE THE CHEESE

1 Place whole fruits—not skinned or topped and tailed—into a large pan. Cover with the water and stew slowly until tender and pulpy.

2 Pour through a sieve into a jug to siphon off any excess juice. Depending on the type of fruit used, there might be a lot or only a little.

3 Place the sieve with the slushy fruit back over the pan and use a wooden spoon to press pulp through the sieve, leaving behind the skins and seeds. Occasionally scrape the underside of the sieve with a spoon to unclog if need be. When no more pulp is coming through, discard the hard mass of skin and seeds.

4 Pour up to 225ml (8 fl. oz.) of the siphoned off juice back into the pan and mix with the pulp. Set the rest aside for use in cocktails, jellies or cordials.

5 Measure the pulp mixture in a jug and place 450g (1 lb.) of sugar for every 600ml (1 pt.) of pulp in the pan. Heat gently until the sugar is dissolved, stirring all the while with a wooden spoon.

6 Simmer until the fruit is very thick, about 15–30 minutes. When the mixture doesn't rush back to cover the line your spoon makes on the bottom of the pan, it's ready.

7 Pour into heart-shaped ramekin dishes and cover with a heart shape of wax paper. When cool, add a tight cellophane cover and leave in a cool, dark place until needed.

8 To serve, turn out molds like a blancmange on a small plate. Lightly oil one side of your stencil so it won't stick. Place the stencil on the cheese and lightly dust through the design with edible gold powder on a large, soft brush. Remove stencil carefully.

PANTRY PERFECTIONS

These tips may assist in your fruit cheese making endeavours!

· Wiping a little glycerine around the inside of your molds will help the fruit unmold cleanly and easily.

· If you have been making fruit jellies by extracting and using just the juice, you can make fruit cheese with all the leftover pulp to avoid waste.

· In place of a sieve, you can use a passata maker (or food mill) to quickly and easily press the pulp, leaving the seeds and skin behind.

Time Traveler's Tart

The longevity of the inhabitants of Shangri-La has been a matter of debate among the Natural Philosophical Society for many years. It has been suggested that it might be the fresh mountain air, that the glacial stream running through the area is, in fact, the fountain of youth, or that a chronology re-location device allows the populace to hop back and forth so frequently that the universe has gotten confused and given up on trying to age them.

This sweet tart filling is softened by the addition of cream and fruit, and it's guaranteed to lure the most hardened temporal adventurer home to tea.

Ingredients

FOR THE PASTRY

100g (3½ oz.) butter

175g (6 oz.) plain flour

10ml (2 tsp.) of water

FOR THE FILLING

175g (6 oz.) tin of evaporated milk

55g (2 oz.) dark brown sugar

100g (3½ oz.) light brown sugar

1 egg

5ml (1 tsp.) vanilla extract

FOR DECORATION

Small tub double cream (whipped until it holds its shape)

Blueberries

TO MAKE THE PASTRY

1 Preheat the oven to gas mark 4 (350° F/180° C) and grease a deep 7" (18cm) loose-bottomed flan tin.

2 Rub the fat into the flour until it resembles bread crumbs. Keep rubbing until it just starts to clump together.

3 Add a few drops of water and mix until the mixture holds together and forms a ball of dough. The less water you can get away with adding, the tastier the pastry will be!

4 Leave the pastry to rest for roughly 10 minutes, then roll out to approximately ⅛" (3mm) thickness on a floured board. Place the pastry in the greased tin and trim neatly. Prick all over with a fork.

5 Line the pastry with parchment or grease-proof paper, then fill with baking beans and bake blind for 15 minutes. Allow to cool.

PANTRY PERFECTIONS

If time is of the essence, you could make this tart using a shop-bought pastry case.
For pretty individual portions, create tiny tarts using a jam tart tin and bake for 10 minutes. However, you need a fairly deep pastry case or the proportion of filling to tart isn't quite right.
The fruit really does add the finishing touch of both flavor and color to this tart, if you can't find blueberries, try mulberries or blackberries instead.

129

For the Filling

1 Turn the oven up to gas mark 5 (375° F/190° C). Sift the sugars together to get rid of any lumps and set aside.

2 Next, mix the evaporated milk with an electric whisk for 3–4 minutes until thick and fluffy. Your mixture should resemble double cream.

3 Add the sugar to your mixture and whisk again for 3–4 minutes until blended. Whisk in the egg and vanilla extract to finish the filling.

4 Pour the filling into the pastry case. Bake for 15–20 minutes, or just until the middle doesn't wobble when you shake the tin.

5 Allow the tart to cool in the tin.

To Decorate

1 Remove the fully cooled tart from the pan and place on a serving plate.

2 Smooth the whipped cream across the top of the tart and add a whirling vortex of blueberries as a finishing touch.

THE PASHA'S CHAI

TO MAKE THE CHAI

1 Crack the cloves, peppercorns and cardamoms in a pestle and mortar, just enough to release the flavor.

2 Bring the cinnamon, ginger and tea to a boil in the water for just one minute.

3 Add the milk and bring to a boil, then remove from heat, strain through a fine sieve and add sugar to taste. (You can retain the spice mix and tea to create a second serving later).

Ingredients

300ml (½ pt.) water

225ml (8 fl. oz.) milk

5 cardamom pods

10 black peppercorns

1 stick cinnamon

5 cloves

10g (2 tsp.) loose black tea

5g (1 tsp.) grated fresh ginger

5–15g (1–3 tsp.) sugar, depending on taste.

SHERPA'S CHESTNUTS

The French mountaineer Marguerite Mont-Blanc once survived two weeks in a Yeti's cave during a blizzard. On her public speaking tour, she explained how she had kept the ferocious beasts at bay by sharing her favorite Marrons Glacé and entertaining them with shadow shows.

More reminiscent of soft and chewy candied fruits than crunchy nut brittle, this fragrant treat was soon adopted by the local mountain guides and rangers, who added their own spices to the mix. The resulting sweets are delicious with strong Turkish coffee, while the three days they take to make has turned into a public holiday of storytelling, where outrageous tales of derring-do are bandied back and forth.

Ingredients

225g (8 oz.) cooked and shelled marron quality chestnuts (or a small tin of cooked ones)

225g (8 oz.) sugar

225ml (8 fl. oz.) water

Cinnamon stick

5 cardamom pods

FOR DECORATION

Gold leaf or edible gold glitter

Special Supplies

Paper cases

Sugar thermometer

PANTRY PERFECTIONS

You'll need a sugar thermometer to get the temperature just right for these. I use a spoon that has a thermometer set into the handle, making things very easy.

You may find that the sugar crystallizes while the chestnuts are soaking. It's a good idea to put everything in a heatproof bowl and microwave the crystallized mixture for 30 seconds to 1 minute before transferring to the pan again, just so the sugar can melt and you don't have to chip it out of the bowl!

TO MAKE THE CHESTNUTS

1 Place water in a pan. Melt the sugar in the water, stirring until it reaches 212° F (100° C). Add cinnamon and cardamom and simmer for 5 minutes.

2 Add chestnuts and simmer for another 10 minutes between 212–225° F (100–110° C). Allow to cool a little, then transfer to a small bowl and leave to soak for 12–18 hours.

3 Return everything (chestnuts and syrup) to a clean pan. Heat and simmer for 2 minutes. Cool a little, then return to a bowl to soak for another 12 hours.

4 Repeat the heating, simmering and soaking for a third time, then remove the cinnamon stick and cardamom seeds.

5 Heat for a fourth time, then lift the chestnuts out with a fork one by one, lightly draining each chestnut before placing it on an oiled baking tray.

6 Place the tray in a very cool oven for around 30 minutes or until the chestnuts are dry to the touch.

7 Decorate with gold leaf and place in paper cases to serve.

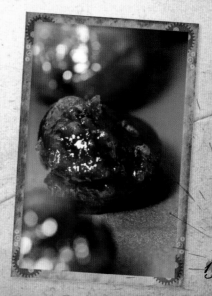

HOUSEKEEPER'S PERKS

Marron quality is a larger type of chestnut. Of course, you can make these treats with any kind of chestnut you have available, but using the larger marron quality makes for easier peeling.

To cook the chestnuts for this recipe, you need to boil them. Make a slit in the skins and drop them into a pan of boiling water for 10 minutes. Transfer the chestnuts to a pan of cold water. When cool enough to touch, carefully peel the chestnuts, removing the hard outer case and the soft, papery inner membrane. Set each golden nut aside. Note that chestnuts are easier to peel while still a little warm.

To roast your own chestnuts, cut a ½" (1.3cm) slit in each shell so they will not burst when heated. Place on the edge of an open fire, on a small fire-proof shovel or in a special chestnut roaster tin. Cook over the fire, shaking or turning frequently for about 10 minutes or until the skin is nearly black. Cool for a few minutes, peel and eat.

If open flames are not readily available, you can also place them in a single layer in a shallow tin and bake at gas mark 6 (400° F/200° C) for 30 minutes.

PEAR PARSNIP AND ROSE LOAF CAKE

The fruit and vegetables are wonderfully abundant in Shangri-La . . . sometimes a little too abundant, leading to a glut of one type or another. Many inventions have been created to run on the surplus, including a carrot-propelled ornithopter and a peach-propelled bicycle. Much experimentation takes place as travelers arrive from the outside world with new and exciting seeds or spices.

Some are more willing to experiment than others, of course. When the ingredients of this healthful pudding were pointed out, Mr. Rivet was heard to mutter, "It barely deserves the name cake!" He then managed to devour three slices and looked disappointed that there was none left for breakfast.

Ingredients

FOR THE CAKE

2 large pears

90ml (6 tbsp.) rosewater

10ml (2 tsp.) apple cider vinegar

85ml (3 fl. oz.) unsweetened soya milk

140g (5 oz.) self-rising gluten-free flour
(I use Doves Farm rice/potato/tapioca/
buckwheat blend)

60g (2 oz.) dried polenta

10g (2 tsp.) baking powder

15g (1 tbsp.) granulated stevia

115g (4 oz.) grated raw parsnip

30ml (1 fl. oz.) oil

2.5g (½ tsp.) bicarbonate of soda (baking
soda)

FOR DECORATION

Edible gold leaf

Rose-flavored butter icing (optional)

PANTRY PERFECTIONS

This vegan, gluten-free, sugar-free, low-fat cake is quite different in texture and taste compared to an ordinary sponge cake; it's almost more like a subtly sweet and dense pudding cake. Feel free to substitute wheat flour for the gluten-free variety if you prefer a spongier texture. You can also use sugar rather than stevia if you're not fussed about that, either!

136

TO MAKE THE CAKE

1 Preheat the oven to gas mark 6 (400° F/200° C). Cut the pears in half and remove the cores. Place cut side down in a shallow baking dish and cover with rosewater. Bake for 30 minutes.

2 Remove the pears from the oven and allow to cool until you can handle them without burning yourself. In the meantime, lower the oven temperature to gas mark 5 (375° F/190° C) and line a loaf tin with grease-proof paper.

3 Once the pears are cool enough to handle, gently remove the skin. Cut one entire pear and half of the other into ¼"–½" (6mm–1.3cm) cubes and set aside. The remaining half of a pear can be thinly sliced and served alongside the cake.

4 Add the vinegar to the soya milk and leave to curdle for a few minutes.

5 In a separate bowl, mix the flour, polenta, baking powder and stevia together.

6 Add the grated parsnip to the cubed pears and mix well, being careful not to mash the pears.

7 Add the oil and bicarbonate of soda to the curdled soya milk and mix well. Pour the oil/milk mixture and the parsnip/pear mixture into the dry ingredients, folding together gently. Blend until all the ingredients are incorporated, once again being careful not to squash the pear pieces.

8 Pour the batter into the lined tin and bake for about 45 minutes or until the cake is golden and springs back when pressed in the center.

9 Leave to cool in the tin for 5 minutes then turn out onto a wire rack.

10 When cold, press edible gold leaf all over the cake and decorate with rose-flavored butter icing flowers if you like. Serve in chunky slices.

HOUSEKEEPER'S PERKS

For the luscious rose-flavored icing, you will
need the following:
· 50g (1³/₄ oz.) unsalted butter
· 15ml (1 tbsp.) rose cordial or a few drops of
flavored essence (rosewater doesn't work well
with butter icing)
· 1–3 drops of pink food coloring
· 80g (3 oz.) icing sugar

Beat the butter until light and fluffy.
Add the pink coloring and flavoring to the
icing sugar one drop at a time, then beat this
mixture into the butter.
Put in a piping bag and swirl roses on the
cake. Follow my YouTube instructions to learn
how to pipe roses!
Obviously, butter icing isn't vegan. You can use
margarine as a substitute, but the flavor won't
be as rich. As such, if you want a quick vegan
icing, I'd suggest simply adding a 15ml (1 tbsp.)
of rosewater to 40g (1¹/₂ oz.) of icing sugar and
drizzling it over the top of the cake instead.

Resources

MOST OF THE THINGS YOU NEED FOR THE RECIPES IN THIS BOOK YOU WILL ALREADY HAVE IN YOUR KITCHEN: WEIGHING SCALES, BOWLS, WOODEN SPOONS, ETC.

I demonstrate several basic techniques on my YouTube channel: www.youtube.com/jemahewitt.

These are a number of specialist suppliers for the more unusual ingredients and decorations:

· The brass Steampunk gear wheel stencil used on the Gooseberry and Blackcurrant Cheese is from Dreamweaver Stencils: www.dreamweaverstencils.com

· The custom-etched scientific glass wear and test tubes for the cocktails are from Etsy: www.etsy.com/shop/EtchedinTimeLLC

· Stripey Syringe Push Pop containers and cake pop sticks are available from assorted Etsy vendors: www.etsy.com

· The rubber stamp used on the Gingerbread Woppits is from www.paperartsy.co.uk

· Fine Tea is supplied by the East India Company: www.theeastindiacompany.com

· Cake Decorating supplies (including candy melts) are from Wilton and Squires Shop: www.wilton.com and www.squires-shop.com

TO FIND OUT MORE ABOUT STEAMPUNK, ONLINE COMMUNITIES AND FORUMS ARE A GREAT PLACE TO START

· Brass goggles forum, blog and worldwide information
www.brassgoggles.co.uk#

· The Victorian Steampunk Society (UK)
www.thevss.yolasite.com

· Steamcon Steampunk convention:
www.steamcon.org

· Online Steampunk magazine:
http://steampunkchronicle.com

There are many Steampunk-related Facebook groups, too, including *Steampunk*, *The British Steampunk Community* and, of course, Emilly Ladybird's own page www.facebook.com/emillyladybird.

Oven Temperature Conversions

GAS MARK	°C	°F
¼	110	225
½	120–130	250
1	140	275
2	150	300
3	160–170	325
4	180	350
5	190	375
6	200	400
7	220	425
8	230	450
9	240	475

Dry Goods Weights and Measures

GRAMS	OUNCES
10	¼
15	½
30	1
60	2
90	3
125	4 (¼ lb.)
155	5
185	6
220	7
250	8 (½ lb.)
280	9
315	10
345	11
375	12 (¾ lb.)
410	13
440	14
470	15
500 (½kg)	16 (1 lb.)

Equivalent Cup Weights and Measures

INGREDIENT	1 CUP EQUIVALENT
Butter	250g, 8 oz.
Cheese, shredded or grated	80g, 2½ oz.
Chocolate bits	190g, 6 oz.
Flour, plain/self-rising	150g, 4¾ oz.
Brown sugar, lightly packed	160g, 5 oz.
Sugar, caster	220g, 7 oz.
Sugar, icing	150g, 4¾ oz.
Sugar, white	225g, 7 oz.
Sultanas	170g, 5½ oz.

Liquid Measures

METRIC	CUP	IMPERIAL
30ml		1 fl. oz.
60ml	¼ cup	2 fl. oz.
80ml	⅓ cup	2¾ fl. oz.
100ml		3½ fl. oz.
125ml	½ cup	4 fl. oz.
150ml		5 fl. oz.
180ml	¾ cup	6 fl. oz.
200ml		7 fl. oz.
250ml	1 cup	8¾ fl. oz.

BIOGRAPHIES

JEMA *Emilly Ladybird* HEWITT, AUTHOR

Among the many extraordinary and unusual jobs Jema pursued before writing took hold was that of wedding cake designer and decorator. Her devotion to culinary perfection is second only to her pursuit of the ideal corset as she toils in her little studio, making beautiful things from fabric, beads, wire and string, as well as cake and icing. Her work is exhibited in museums and galleries across Great Britain, and she has a large international fan base among the Steampunk and altered art communities.

"Emilly Ladybird" is Jema's Steampunk alter ego, who leads a terribly exciting life, hunting down treasures for auctioneers Dickens and Rivett while attending parties with leading figures from Victorian history and fiction.

You can find out lots more at www.steampunkjewellery.co.uk. Emilly also has her own Facebook fan page at *www.facebook.com/emillyladybird.*

TERRY LIGHTFOOT, DIGITAL ARTIST

Terry is a virtual chameleon living somewhere between the real world and the digital. Her love of art and all things Victoriana means she mainly inhabits a world of airships, dingoes, time machines and California sunsets.

Like all artists, she lives in a garret, surviving on a diet of absinthe and paella, with a very understanding husband and her K9 pal Cassidy.

She studied fine art at USC and currently focuses her creativity on digital design and artwork.

Peruse her creations at *http://terrylightfoot. wordpress.com.*

MARTIN SOULSTEALER, PHOTOGRAPHER

Soulstealer Photography began life in the primordial soup of the alternative scene in London, documenting the unique and beautifully creative people who frequented the darkest corners of the Capital. Steampunk bubbled to the surface with a Vampire vs. Steampunks event; Soulstealer took the side of the 'punks and he never looked back. The name "Soulstealer" comes from the Victorian superstition that your captured image is a reflection of your soul.

The inventiveness and enthusiasm for a time and set of mores that never really existed never ceases to amaze Martin; the way that translates into costumes, gadgets and, of course, food and drink—all produced by the most civilised bunch of folk you could ever meet—means he is unlikely to ever grow out of this new obsession.

Explore his world at *http://soulstealer.co.uk.*

fw media
www.fwmedia.com

17 16 15 14 13 · 5 4 3 2 1

DISTRIBUTED IN CANADA BY
FRASER DIRECT
100 Armstrong Avenue
Georgetown, ON, Canada L7G 5S4
Tel: (905) 877-4411

DISTRIBUTED IN THE U.K. AND
EUROPE BY DAVID & CHARLES
Brunel House, Newton Abbot, Devon,
TQ12 4PU, England
Tel: (+44) 1626 323200, Fax: (+44) 1626
323319
Email: mail@davidandcharles.co.uk

DISTRIBUTED IN AUSTRALIA BY
CAPRICORN LINK
P.O. Box 704, S. Windsor NSW, 2756
Australia
Tel: (02) 4560-1600
Fax: (02) 4577-5288
books@capricornlink.com.au

ISBN: 978-1-4402-3295-4
SRN: U0178

METRIC CONVERSION CHART

TO CONVERT	TO	MULTIPLY BY
Inches	Centimeters	2.54
Centimeters	Inches	0.4
Feet	Centimeters	30.5
Centimeters	Feet	0.03
Yards	Meters	0.9
Meters	Yards	1.1

EDITOR: LAYNE VANOVER

DESK EDITOR: NOEL RIVERA

DESIGNER: KELLY O'DELL

PHOTOGRAPHER:
MARTIN SOULSTEALER

DIGITAL ARTIST: TERRY LIGHTFOOT

PHOTOGRAPHY STYLIST:
JEMA HEWITT

SOME GRAPHIC ELEMENTS FROM
WWW.ECLECTICANTHOLOGY.COM

DEDICATION

For Ma, Pa and Roz with happy memories of Sunday afternoons at the Penguin Cafe.

ACKNOWLEDGEMENTS

Enormous thanks and glacé cherries to all my models.

All Aboard the Airship *Elegance*: Rebecca, Willoughby, Vincent, Kit, Esther and Jules.

The Scientific Chateau: Ceejay, Simon, Cecile, Phil and Heather.

A Curious Picnic: Bronwyn, Chris, Jeanette and Callecia.

Regimental Lunar Encampment on Mars: Scott, Gina, Dave, Vincent, Alice, Elsie and Max.

Voyage From the Deeps: Ron, Jameela, Darren, Jo, Eddie, James, Ratty, Lydia and George.

Blossoms in Shangri-La: Leanna, Lyssa, Nicolette, Mathew, Ian, Rebecca and Claire.

Also, much appreciation to all who tried the recipes and gave such excellent and often amusing advice and assistance, especially Chief Engineer Hewitt, Nik, Sarah, Sally, Miss Peacey, Lesley and Roland, Kim, Helen, Matt and Kate, and the Families Emmas-Wright and Barnet!

INDEX